MW01107269

Cracked at Birth: One Madcap Mom's Thoughts on Motherhood, Marriage & Burnt Meatloaf

by

Kathryn S. Mahoney

Wyatt-MacKenzie Publishing, Inc.
DEADWOOD, OREGON

CRACKED AT BIRTH:
One Madcap Mom's Thoughts on
Motherhood, Marriage & Burnt Meatloaf
by Kathryn S. Mahoney

ALL RIGHTS RESERVED
© 2005 Kathryn S. Mahoney
ISBN: 1-932279-19-9
Library of Congress Control Number: 2005933303

Illustrations by Ken Kimball
Cover design by Kathryn S. Mahoney
Photo by Briggs Photographics

Published by The Mom-Writers Publishing Cooperative
Wyatt-MacKenzie Publishing, Inc., Deadwood, OR
www.WyMacPublishing.com (541) 964-3314

Requests for permission or further information should be addressed to:
Wyatt-MacKenzie Publishing, 15115 Highway 36, Deadwood, Oregon 97430

Printed in the United States of America

Cracked at Birth:
One Madcap Mom's
Thoughts on
Motherhood, Marriage
& Burnt Meatloaf

Table of Contents

Acknowledgements

There are many people who have helped me realize my dream of writing this book and I would like to take this opportunity to say "thank you."

To my husband, Michael, and sons, Tyler and Andrew, for their unconditional love and permission to write about all of our family foibles. May the word "payback" be absent from your vocabulary in the years to come.

To my parents, Audrey and John, for believing in me no matter what path I chose.

To my sister, Karen, for being my sounding board and an impeccable proofreader.

To the rest of my family and friends, who put up with me and laughed at my jokes even when they weren't that funny.

To Gina, who shares my love of Erma Bombeck, and encouraged me to try my hand at writing a humor column.

To my newspaper editor, Kate, for giving me my "big break" and hiring me as a humor columnist.

To my buddy, Scott, at CreationProject, Inc., for his artistic talent and assistance in creating the cover of this book and designing my Web site (www.crackedatbirth.com).

To my humor writing group, for encouragement and wisdom.

To my publisher, Nancy, for educating me on the wonderful world of publishing and providing me with the tools to succeed.

To the other women of the Mom-Writers Publishing Cooperative at Wyatt-MacKenzie Publishing, Inc., for sharing their experiences during this process and answering all of my silly questions.

And finally, a special thank you to my grandmother, Leona Dent, for passing along her gift of writing and love of the written word. I love and miss you dearly.

Introduction

As I look back through the old shoeboxes stacked in my attic full of letters from camp, articles in the school newspaper, and notebooks of miscellaneous doodles, it is apparent that I have always been trying to write or draw something that would make people laugh. I remember in high school when I really wanted to become a comedienne, and while other girls were dreaming about David Cassidy and Donny Osmond, I was dreaming about becoming the next Lucille Ball or Carol Burnett.

Unfortunately, when it came time to choose a major in college, I didn't have the guts to pursue acting, so I chose the next best thing, a major in broadcasting and learning about everything that happens behind the camera. After college, I produced radio and television commercials for a small retail store chain and then found myself taking a variety of jobs in marketing. The common thread throughout my career, and life, has been using words and pictures to tell a story.

After the birth of my second child in 2000, I decided it was time to leave corporate America and start the next chapter of my own life story—life as a stay-at-home mother. Although my husband was very supportive of my decision, he also reminded me of some of those minor everyday details, like paying the mortgage and buying food. Details, details! To put his mind at rest, I started a marketing communications business out of our home to help with the proverbial bottom line.

After the first year of juggling the demands of raising our two sons and running my business, I decided I needed some comic relief at the end of an otherwise hectic day. I looked back over the day and tried to find the humor in the fact that my son had spewed green peas all over the front of my shirt, and that I had stepped on the deceased chipmunk the cat left on our doorstep. Fortunately, I was able to do so, and wrote these entertaining stories down in my journal. Each night I would make an entry and read what I had written the night before. It didn't take long before I was laughing out loud and my family was staring at me like I had lost my mind. Then, I had an idea. Maybe these stories could help relieve the stress of other stay-at-home mothers.

I strung some of my journal entries into a couple of columns and submitted them to our local newspaper and lo and behold, the editor liked them. In the fall of 2001, I introduced my column, "Sunny Side Up," to the readers of the six newspapers published by Nashoba Publishing of Devens, MA, and have been writing for them ever since.

This book is a compilation of my columns over the past four years. I hope you enjoy reading them as much as I have enjoyed writing them.

Kathryn

Kathryn S. Mahoney

Chapter 1
Honey, I Burned the Meatloaf—AGAIN!

Over the years, I have been known to do things that, let's just say, the average Harvard grad probably wouldn't do. Essentially, my brain suddenly malfunctions and all brain activity comes to a screeching halt. For example, on several occasions I've put dinner in the oven, forgotten to set the timer, and am rudely jolted back to reality not only by the screeching sound of the smoke detector, but also by the unmistaken odor of burnt meatloaf billowing through my kitchen. Some people might get upset over something like this. I guess it happens to me so often that I've made the decision to just laugh (and write) about all of my funny little blunders. Hopefully, after reading the following columns, you'll be able to laugh at your own "burnt meatloaf" moments. Enjoy!

One Ring Circus

"It's a boy!" my husband shouted with glee.

"10 fingers, 10 toes?" I asked in anticipation.

"Yup, and he's a big guy, 8 lbs. 8 oz," the nurse informed.

"Wow. That is big."

And where do big babies come from? Big mommies, of course. I had managed to pack on forty pounds during my second pregnancy and taken a few liberties and a few extra french fries while I was pregnant.

I planned to spend the next three months bonding with my son, and as he continued to gain weight, fortunately, I continued to lose. Each day, I felt a little thinner and around week eight I noticed a slightly thinner frame in the mirror. At the same time, I also noticed something glistening on my dresser. Upon closer inspection, I realized it was the sunlight reflecting off my diamond wedding ring that hadn't encircled my finger in months.

I stared at it for a moment. "Hmmm, I bet I can get this on now."

The ring went over the top part of my finger with no problem. I gave it a little push to get it past my knuckle, knowing the bottom of my finger must certainly be a smaller circumference.

"OOh! C'mon, c'mon. (push, push). Ugh! There."

Well, the ring certainly made it past my knuckle, but within seconds, the skin on my finger was turning purple and hanging over the wedding band like the belly of an overweight man in pants two sizes too small.

"Oh my gosh, maybe this wasn't such a great idea. I gotta get this off."

I grabbed the slimiest lotion I could find and as I lathered it on, my cat stared at me in disbelief, surely thinking, "stupid human."

"Oh, man, what am I going to do now?" I ran downstairs and threw open the freezer door.

"Ice. Yeah, ice. If I put ice on my finger, the swelling will go down, and I'll be able to pull the ring off."

By this time, my finger was as purple as the stuffed Barney lying next to my peacefully sleeping son. I'm sure if he were awake he would have already reached for the closest Fisher Price phone to call a lawyer claiming he was switched at birth.

"Oh, man. This isn't working. What am I going to do?"

I had no other choice. I reached for the phone and dialed 911.

"You what?" was the response on the other end.

"Well, I sorta got my wedding band stuck on my finger. I need someone to cut it off."

"OK, we'll send somebody right over." (Giggle, giggle, click.)

Suddenly, my biggest fear was no longer the throbbing finger dangling from my hand, but the questions I was going to have to answer after my neighbors saw a fire truck with screaming sirens entering our rural neighborhood.

Fortunately, the volunteer fireman who responded was driving a small white van with "Joe's Heating & Plumbing" written on the side. I opened the door and staring back at me was a slight man in coveralls grinning from ear to ear. He could have been an axe murderer for all I knew, but at that point, that almost seemed like a better option, so I let him in.

"I hear you have a little problem," he said with a chuckle.

"Yeah, you could say that," I said as I "gave him the finger."

"Do you think you can get this off?"

"Well, I'll give it a try."

He pulled out some sort of tool, slid it under my ring, and within seconds, I was, "free at last." I walked him to the door knowing full well he was going to race back and tell his buddies about this crazy woman, but at that point I just didn't care.

So, what's happened since? I've lost most of the weight, the ring has been repaired, and my now five-year old son loves to tell the story about when Mommy was the fat lady, ran around like a clown, was stared down by a lion, and saved by the ringmaster. It's a story about a one-ring circus *neither* of us will ever forget.

Super Mom vs. the Super Glue

"Andrew, you better drop that," my eldest warned.

CRASH! "You told me to drop it."

"WAAAAAAAHHHHHH!"

"Andrew!"

"I'm sorry, Mommy. I'm really, really, sorry."

And so it went. My youngest son just broke the horn off the freshly painted kiln-fired rhinoceros my eldest son created in art class. Before you knew it, both of them were sobbing uncontrollably and I just happened to blurt out, "Don't worry, I can fix it."

What was I thinking? This precarious little creature didn't have a chance, but I wanted to be the "Super Mom with the Super Glue." I brought the fractured rhino over to the kitchen and proceeded to attack.

"OK, a drop here, a drop there." I said to myself. As I stood there gluing the horn in place, I realized something else was glued in place. "Oh, shoot."

"What's wrong, Mommy?"

"I just glued my finger to the rhino."

"Oh."

"Hey, Andrew, wanna play dinosaurs?"

"Yeah."

Obviously, my predicament was of no concern to my offspring. I was on my own. Slowly I pulled my finger and watched the skin stretch between the rhino and the finger it was attached to. I admired the tenacity of my opponent, but knew I had to work hard to make it release its grip. Soon, I was free, but left with Super Glue residue on my fingers that had already started to harden. When I tried to wash it off, the water slid off my fingers like the sweat falling from my brow.

"Yuck, I give up."

"What's wrong, Mommy?"

"I can't get the glue off my fingers."

"Oh."

"Hey, Andrew, wanna play Ninja Turtles?"

"Yeah."

I turned back to the rhino and the dreaded tube of Super Glue lying on the counter. I wasn't ready to throw in the towel yet. "Oh, no."

"What's wrong, Mommy?"

"The glue got all over the counter. What a mess."

"Oh."

"Hey, Andrew, wanna watch *SpongeBob*?"

"Yeah."

Speaking of sponges, I grabbed a sponge and started to attack the sticky counter. I was getting nowhere fast, but knew if I didn't take care of it right away, we were doomed. Unfortunately, all the sponge did was smear the glue on the counter so I flung it aside and tag teamed with the paper towels. "Oh, man."

"What's wrong, Mommy?"

"Now the paper towel is stuck to the counter."

"Oh."

"Hey, Andrew, wanna build Legos?"

"Yeah."

Before the trash talk started flying, I remembered my counter was made of Corian and I had a selection of special sandpaper for times like this when Super Moms were confronted by stupid glue, I mean Super Glue. To the wayside went the towels and in came the sandpaper for the final smack down. With a little elbow grease, I started scrubbing. CRASH! Apparently, the sandpaper was a little too much for the rhino. I watched, as if in slow motion, the rhino endured a body slam to the floor. I heard a loud cracking noise and realized it was the sound of a leg and the previously fractured horn breaking away from the rhino. It was a devastating set back.

All of a sudden, all eyes were on me. "Mommy, look what you did. You said you were going to fix it, not break it."

"I know, honey. I tried, but I had a little bit of trouble. I bet Daddy can do it. He can fix anything."

"OK."

Somewhat discouraged, but mostly relieved, I relinquished my title—and the Super Glue. I offered my husband some parting advice. "Watch out for the finger hold, never turn your back on your opponent, and for goodness sake, take it outside."

Good luck, Super Dad! You're going to need it.

What Windshield Wipers?

Is it just me, or do a lot of people go into a state of panic when they get their car inspected? I don't know what happens to me. I've been driving for 21 years now (I got my license when I was 8) and I have no marks on my license. So, basically I'm a competent driver, but when I enter that inspection station, my brain stays behind in the parking lot.

This year, I decided to give myself a little pep talk before pulling into the inspection station. "OK, don't choke. You can do this. It's no big deal. Don't panic." All of a sudden, I had a flashback of last year's inspection when I "restarted" my engine while it was running and it made that lovely scraping sound. The time before that, I pulled a Chevy Chase from the movie *Vacation* and put the car in drive instead of reverse as I was looking over my shoulder to exit the garage. I tried telling myself these bad experiences were about to come to an end. It was time.

I entered the first bay of the inspection garage very slowly, staring straight ahead as if in a trance. The technician motioned me forward and I could tell he started to say something, but I couldn't hear what he was saying. I leaned over to stick my head out the window and suddenly I felt a shooting pain crashing through my skull. Why? I had just slammed my head against the closed window. "Argh," I said to myself. "It's already begun."

Calmly, after almost taking the guy out at the kneecaps, I rolled down my window and realized he was simply saying, "Stop." I stopped the car, handed him my registration and inspection fee, and thought to myself, "OK, things are going well." He processed the information in that weird looking inspection machine and was ready to proceed with the test.

"Blow your horn." Fine. "Turn on your lights." Pass. "Flash your high beams." Well done. "Turn on your windshield wipers." Panic. Shear panic. What windshield wipers? Do I have windshield wipers? I think I got ripped off. My minivan didn't come with windshield wipers. It's an outrage. Then, I see this hand reach into the driver's side and casually turn this stick like object extending from my steering wheel.

"Oh, those windshield wipers," I say to him with a smile. I can see him in my rearview mirror, chuckling and shaking his head.

I just can't figure out what happens to me. I consider myself fairly intelligent. I have a master's degree. I'm a professional. But something about this process makes me prove the stereotypical depiction of, well, a blonde. (I can say that because I am a blonde. Although these days, more of a chemically enhanced blonde.) But seriously, what happens to my brain when I get my car inspected? Perhaps it's the fumes? Perhaps I just don't test well? Maybe they should make provisions for people like me. I wonder if we can do car inspections online?

Well, I'm not going to lose hope. Someday soon this run of bad visits to the inspection station will come to an end. If not, I'll hire a stunt double to do the inspection. All I can say is, thank goodness it only comes once a year.

Airing Dirty Laundry

"Warm wash lights." "Warm wash darks." "Cold wash lights." "Cold wash darks." "Hand wash mild soap." "Dry clean only." What—are you kidding?

Did you ever notice how many instructions there are to wash clothing? It's mind-boggling. At our house, there are two types of laundry—dirty and clean. The dirty sits in the hamper until we can't find the cat that has been buried in the overflow, and the clean sits on the hope chest in our bedroom hoping to be put away.

My sister has five separate categories for her laundry. She says she developed this system because of one shirt that was ruined from incorrect washing. I can't be bothered with such details. I've been washing darks in cold and lights in warm for as long as I've been doing laundry. Sure, my husband has had to wear an occasional pair of pink underwear, but he's a real man, he doesn't care. Heck, he sleeps in a pink room under a rose colored comforter. What's the big deal?

When we were first married and lived in an apartment, we divided the two dreaded chores. He got grocery shopping and I got the laundry. Every two weeks I would pack up our dirty clothes in garbage bags and drag them to the laundromat. At the time, I didn't mind it too much. You could do it all at once and you got some good reading done. However, after being spoiled by having my own washer and dryer, the laundromat was a place I *thought* I would never have to visit again. That was—until my washing machine broke.

Armed with rolls of quarters and loads of dirty duds, I was off to find a laundromat. I found one in a neighboring town and, believe it or not, it was a sight for sore eyes. I flung open the doors to my minivan and started the laundromat march. In with two laundry baskets, back for two duffel bags, back again for two more duffel bags and finally, the giant jug of laundry soap.

Everything seemed so foreign. I didn't have a clue how much the washers cost, which ones to use, where to put the soap, or anything. Apparently, my ignorance and the fact that I was fumbling over everything revealed my laundromat incompetence to those around me. Or, maybe it was the fact that my industrial size laundry soap was leaking, leaving a slippery trail everywhere I walked.

After inserting a slot machine's supply of quarters into various machines, I had about six loads of laundry going at once. I carefully marked my territory by placing bags and laundry baskets on top of MY washers. When they were done, I headed for the dryers. First, I approached a bank of dryers that seemed to be from the 1950s. After loading about eight quarters into one of them, I realized these things probably stopped working during the days of Elvis. Once again, the "regulars" were staring at me and shaking their heads. I decided waiting for the 21st century dryers was a better solution and after about two hours, I left the ol' laundromat and vowed never to return.

Finally, on the tenth day after original diagnosis, the repairman not only fixed my washing machine, but also gave me a tip that you're supposed to add water when adding fabric softener. He felt the need to explain this after pulling apart my washer and showing me the thick blue goo that was caked on the machine. Oops!

When he left, I kissed my new best friend (the washing machine, not the repairman) and promised I would never stuff it with an oversized comforter again. We bonded that day and I haven't complained about doing laundry since.

Well, maybe just a little.

Help Yourself

I've been thinking about moving my bookcase and books from my office to the living room to create some more space in my office. However, after scanning the bookshelf and noticing that most of the books are "self-help" or "how to" books, I decided to leave everything where it is. All I could envision was people coming over to my house, looking at the books, looking back at me, and wondering, "Hmm—did it work?"

Truth is, some of them worked, some of them are collecting dust, and some are a work in progress. Here's the breakdown:

Self-Help

Secrets of Power Persuasion – Nah, I'm still not very persuasive. I still pay full sticker price at the car dealership.

Living the 7 Habits – What were they again?

Keeping Your Cool Under Fire – Definitely didn't work. I still have the German temper I was born with, magnified by the stubborn streak bestowed upon me by being born under the sign of Taurus the bull. Not a good combination.

Awaken the Giant Within – She's still sleeping.

Next…

How-To Books

How to Start a Home-Based Desktop Publishing Business – Score! As of 2000, I have been successfully running my own marketing communications business.

How to Do Leaflets, Newspapers, and Newsletters – Yep! Doing it.

How to Train for a Marathon – Well, I got up to 13 miles in my training and then called it quits. Basically, after running 2 1/2 hours I got bored and was thinking about all of the things I should be doing. You know, like folding clothes and cleaning out my sock drawer?

OK things are looking up. What's next?

Raising Kids

Right Brained Children in a Left Brained World – I actually traded my copy of *Sensory Integration Dysfunction* for this one. My friend, another self-help junkie, and I were both trying our hand at armchair psychology to diagnose our children's idiosyncrasies. Fortunately for our kids, we decided to leave it up to the professionals.

S.O.S. Help for Parents – This is actually on my bedside table and is so dog-eared it's almost unrecognizable. I need all the help I can get.

You Can't Make Me – Oh, yes I can.

The other books that round out my display are *Personal Finance for Dummies* and *Investing for Dummies*. When I was born, God blessed me with creativity, but any financial prowess went to the guy behind me. This explains why I dropped accounting as my major after one semester of college. What was I thinking?

If your books say something about your personality, what does my collection say about me? I guess it says I'm somebody who is always trying to improve herself, her skills, and her kids. That doesn't sound too bad. Maybe I'll move that bookcase into the living room after all.

Take My Gall Bladder—Please

If I had to write a synopsis of, "How I spent my Memorial Day weekend," it would go something like this…

Monday, 1:00 a.m. – Couldn't get to sleep. Felt like Shelley Winters was sitting on my chest. Realizing this scenario was quite unlikely and a little creepy, I decided to call my doctor. He told me to come into the Emergency Room right away.

My sister was visiting, so I woke her to tell her where we were going. Keen to my past hypochondriac ways, she lifted her head off the pillow, looked at me out of the corner of her eye and said, "It's probably just heartburn."

"No way, I think I'm having a heart attack," I said. By this time, she was already back in REM sleep. I looked at my husband and said, "Oprah did a show and said that women are having heart attacks at younger ages. Oprah knows everything." My husband, rolling his eyes, relented, and drove me in.

ER – One of the first things I was asked was, "If you had to rate the pain between one and ten, with ten being the worst, how would you rate it?" What kind of question is that? Let's see, child-birth with no epidural was pretty miserable, where does that rate? Under the pressure, I quickly devised my own pain meter: one = hangnail and ten = slow painful death. With that in mind, I blurted out…"seven."

The Doctor – After a blood test, an EKG, and a quick run to the Ouija board, the doctor said, "I think it's your gall bladder. Call on Tuesday and schedule an ultrasound. Here's a prescription. Good luck."

Nice try, Doc. By noon that same day, we were en route to the Emergency Room again.

eR, Round 2 – As I paced around the waiting room writhing in pain, I noticed that everyone else was calmly reading magazines. What's up with that? Isn't the Emergency Room for people in dire pain? They all looked like they had just stepped off the massage table. Surely, they have to take people with a higher pain rating first. To test my theory, I upgraded my pain to a "nine." I was wrong. I watched as hangnail after hangnail walked past me.

The Doctor – When I finally got to see a doctor, he scheduled an immediate ultrasound.

Apparently, I had a very infected gall bladder and four gall-stones. He informed me, in Wicked Witch of the West fashion, "We're going to remove your gall bladder and your little gall stones, too."

The Surgeon – The surgeon came in to my hospital room that night after I was asleep. As he fumbled for the light switch, he made his way over to my bedside. He was reaching for something in his white hospital coat, and I was hoping, no praying, that this was indeed my surgeon and not a mass murderer reaching for a gun. Although, come to think of it, it would have made an interesting plot for a made-for-TV movie.

"Hi, I'm Dr. Smith. I'm going to perform your operation tomorrow." He started pointing at a laminated picture of a gall bladder and explaining the procedure. Since I was on pain medication, half-asleep and without my glasses, he could have just explained a sex change operation for all I knew. After he left, I rolled over and said a short prayer.

The Surgery – Success. Despite minor incision pain, it was nothing like the pain that put me there in the first place.

The Recovery – With support from my husband, mother, church, neighbors, and friends, my recovery has gone very smoothly. The good news—no more pain. The better news—I've lost five pounds from the whole ordeal and am that much closer to meeting my weight loss goal.

Hmmm, I think I feel appendicitis coming on.

Has Anybody Seen Me?

Have you ever felt like you were invisible? I can't tell you how often I feel that way. I don't know when exactly I became "Transparent Woman," but college conjures up some memories.

I entered college knowing my friend from high school was going to be my roommate. I thought the familiarity would deflect some of the scariness of going away to a new place. What I didn't know was that I would not only be her shadow, but like a fleck of white fuzz on the carpet. You know, you kind of see it, but you walk past it anyway. It was somewhat explainable. She was voted class clown in high school and always had center stage. College was no different. So, I would often overhear conversations that went something like this.

"You know, the blonde girl. She lives on the third floor. You know, Nancy's roommate."

"Oh yeah, Nancy's roommate, now I know who you mean."

Talk about an identity crisis.

This see-through phenomenon happens a lot when I'm out shopping. The other day I was standing in line and a checkout girl opened up her register and declared, "Next, please." I was clearly next in line but the woman behind me boldly walked up to the counter. I pinched myself to make sure I wasn't dreaming and then I wanted to pinch that woman to show her that I clearly wasn't a figment of her imagination. Instead, I just stood there.

Once, I had an experience with my friend, Gina. We attended the Erma Bombeck writing conference in Ohio together and were standing in line for a book signing by a noted comedian and author from Boston. Even though I was wearing a nametag that was practically glowing, the author took my book, looked at me, and wrote, "To Gina, with Love." What's up with that?

I can't figure it out. I don't know if it's because of my fair complexion, because I'm shy, or because my face just blends into whatever I'm standing in front of. You would think as a humor writer I would have a dynamic personality that wouldn't be missed, but I guess I really don't. I've always thought I was funnier on paper, and my neighbor confirmed this theory when she said, "Kathy, I love your column. It's great. But, I gotta tell ya, I never knew you were—well—funny." Not exactly what a humor writer wants to hear, but given my translucent past, not surprising.

I know my kids think I'm invisible. Why else would they ignore me when I'm three inches from their faces, screaming until the veins pop out of my head? They seem to be looking at me, but I swear, they are looking right through me, affixing their eyes on Clifford, the big red dog, on TV. Maybe that's it. Maybe I need to jump into a big vat of red paint and I'll suddenly materialize.

Oh, well. I'm so used to it now, I just laugh about it. But can you do me a favor? If you "find me" around town, can you please stop and say, "Hi, Kath. Love your column. How are you doing?" I'll happily pay you a handsome finder's fee—a smile!

Old, Who's Old?

Last year, I celebrated my 40th birthday. When I was a kid, I thought if you were 40 you already had one foot in the grave. Now that I've reached this milestone, I'd like to say I've changed my opinion, but I'm not really sure I have.

My "advanced age" is most apparent on Monday and Wednesday nights. These are the nights I get together with other elderly gals and play basketball. I feel like Al Bundy from *Married with Children* trying to relive the glory days of my high school basketball career. Sure, I may still have my jump shot, but after each game instead of reaching for H_2O and a towel, I'm reaching for O_2 and a stretcher.

I can't figure it out. In the old days, I was in great shape and relatively injury-free. Since I've been playing in this league, I've suffered a sprained thumb, patella tendonitis, and most recently a pinched nerve in my back. Why do I keep putting my body through this? I'm not quite sure. I think it's a combination of pure stupidity and a pure love of the game. Whatever it is, I'm not alone in my plight. Here's a typical pre-game conversation.

"Hey, Melissa, how's the knee?"

"Not good. I tore my anterior cruciate ligament, I've got to have surgery, and I'll be out nine months."

"Oh, man, that stinks."

"Yeah, how's your back?"

"I've got a pinched nerve. I have to go to a chiropractor for the next four weeks."

"Ouch!"

"Hey Gina, how are you doing?"

"Oh, my ankles are shot. Thanks for lending me your ankle brace. It helps to have one on both ankles."

"Hey, Kris. What's up?"

"The doctor said I could finally get rid of my knee braces. I just hope I don't blow my knee out again."

"Yeah, that would be a drag."

"Hey Cathy, how's the foot?"

"Alright. Turns out it's a stress fracture."

"And your back?"

"Arthritis."

"Bummer."

You know, I've heard that with age comes wisdom, but apparently not when it comes to ex-athletes who are trying to "keep the dream alive." So if you go by the saying, "You're only as old as you feel," I feel like I'm about 90. But, I also believe that life isn't a spectator sport, so despite the pain, I'm going to try and live by the Nike philosophy, "Just do it!"

"Hey guys, I heard they're starting up a women's rugby league in the spring. You wanna play?

{In unison} "I'm in!"

Tales of a NonconFORMist

With the current interest rates being so low, my husband and I were recently weighing the pros and cons of purchasing a new home versus refinancing our current home. Heck, this is the only good thing about our economy right now, so why not take advantage of it, right? We ran the numbers, developed different scenarios, but when all was said and done, it came down to this. Which process requires filling out the least number of forms?

We opted for refinancing. We figured all the bank had to do was change the loan amount, adjust the interest rate, do a little recalculation, and voila. WRONG! Two redwoods later, we're still not finished with the paperwork.

It doesn't help that I suffer from "formophobia." You know, the fear of filling out forms? I don't know what happens, but all of a sudden I feel like a guilty felon living this mysterious life and they're going to "find me out." Truth be told, I'm a pretty straight arrow and never had any run-ins with the law, not even as much as a speeding ticket. So why do I panic? Who knows? Maybe I have a subconscious desire to live life on the lam, or maybe revealing all of this information just makes me feel—well—naked.

For example, the other day I was filling out a form and having these little conversations in my head. "Name. Which name? First name, last name, mother's maiden name? Maybe I should just come up with an alias. Address. Why do they need to know that? Is someone going to stalk me? Phone Number. I'm definitely not putting that. I don't want any weirdos calling me."

With my hand trembling, I slowly pushed the completed form across the desk to the woman requesting it. I stared down at the floor in anticipation, and after what seemed like a lifetime, I heard a voice say, "Thank you Mrs. Pterodactyl. Here's your new library card." Phew! That was close.

So, when I first started the refinancing process, I decided to do it online. For some reason, I find online forms a little less intimidating. I was cruising right along and was on the home stretch when all of a sudden—CRASH! My computer froze. At that point, I knew filling out the forms online wasn't going to be as easy as I had hoped. This became abundantly clear after the THIRD time my computer froze. Fortunately, three times a charm, as I was able to submit the application just before my computer seized for the fourth time. I was DONE! Or, so I thought.

A few days later, I received a package in the mail from the financial institution I had applied to. I was sure it was to notify us everything was all set. WRONG! The envelope was brimming with those nasty, epic length forms I was trying to avoid in the first place. If ever I wanted to cut a vein, it was then. Fortunately (or unfortunately), both my husband and I use electric razors.

I painstakingly filled out the forms, line-by-line, page-by-page. When I was finally finished, I copied them (the copier jammed five times), and trudged to the post office to mail them. I handed the hefty package to the attendant and was about to breathe a sigh of relief when she asked, "Would you like to send this certified or get notification of receipt on this, ma'am?"

Not wanting to repeat this process *ever* again, I haggardly replied, "Yes, please."

"OK. Could you please fill out these three forms?" AAAAAAAAAHHHHHHHHHH!

Dieting, Schmieting

Well, it's bathing suit season again, and I am not happy. No matter how many different suits I try on, there is still one common denominator—I look fat. I'm not sure exactly when all of this extra weight came on, but if pictures are worth 1,000 words, it looks like this downhill spiral started shortly after we got married and picked up speed after the birth of our two children.

Everyone tells you about the freshman ten when you're entering college, but no one happened to mention the post-birth twenty, at least not to me. OK, maybe I took a few liberties while I was pregnant, but I've been exercising and dieting off and on for the past ten years, and nothing seems to keep the weight off. Frankly, I'm tired of having this "baby fat" cuddle up on my lap every time I sit down. "It" seems cozy, but I'm certainly not.

However, despite the disappointments, I'm not giving up. I have a weight loss goal and hope to obtain it sometime between now and my 20th high school reunion. I left there as Class Athlete and I'm determined not to return as Class Fatlete. So, I've been running, playing basketball, lifting weights, doing yoga, eating rice cakes, pretending tofu tastes good, and sniffing chocolate hoping to get the same high as when I engulf a nice big Hershey bar.

I've been looking at all the diet plans out there and decided that I would try an online program. It's a cyberspace diet that provides meal plans and asks you to weigh in online every week. It's good in theory, but I think I need Helga, hovering over me as I stand on a cold metal scale, yelling at me as if I was in weight loss boot camp. Instead, I type in my weight (I'm usually pretty honest) and Cindy Cyberspace types back, "It's OK, Kathy, just cut back a little more and you'll have better luck next week." Somehow, it's just not the same. Besides, *Consumer Reports* just did a study and found that 83% of the people who lost weight and kept it off did so on their own without following any specific diet plan. Maybe someday I'll write my own humorous weight loss book showing how absurd some of these diet programs are. I think I'll call it, *You Won't Lose a Pound, but You'll Laugh Your Butt Off.*

I'll probably never stop dieting, but I'm going to try to not be so hard on myself. I think I'll approach it borrowing the Special Olympics oath, "Let me win. But if I cannot win, let me be brave in the attempt."

Let's look at the facts. We're all going to die someday, no

matter how much we weigh. I'm pretty sure I'll still be able to get into heaven; the angels just might have to hold the gate open a little wider.

Somebody Stop Me

"Hello, my name is Kathy and I'm addicted to real estate."

It's true. I don't know what's wrong with me. I live in a perfectly nice house with a beautifully remodeled kitchen, we have great neighbors and I *still* feel compelled to look at what houses are on the market. It's a sickness. I know it is. But I can't seem to help myself. Please, somebody stop me.

This compulsion seems to come in waves. I'll be OK for awhile and then I'll hear about somebody buying a house and I'll get itchy. Then I'll see a picture of a beautiful house in a magazine and I'll get really itchy. By the time Sunday rolls around, my car becomes a heat-seeking missile when it's within a ten-mile radius of an Open House.

Just the other day, I dragged my kids to an Open House, despite their desperate pleas not to surrender to this addiction. "No, Mommy, no. Please don't make us." With each child tucked under an arm, I entered a beautiful new Cape-style home, smiled at the real estate agent, and headed toward the dining room to sign the guest book. I acted as if I would have no problem coming up with the $850,000 they were asking for this mansion, but somehow, I think she was a little suspicious. I don't know if it was that my boys were scratching the hardwood floors with their dinosaurs, that the vehicle I arrived in was scratched beyond recognition and missing a hubcap, or that I was wearing a ripped T-shirt emblazoned with a skull and crossbones. Oh well, I didn't really care. I needed a fix.

During the week, I quench my thirst for real estate by exploring the depths of the World Wide Web. And what a tangled web it weaves. It starts first thing in the morning when I come downstairs for breakfast. As I head for the kitchen, I walk by the computer and fire it up. Then, in concert with the flow of orange juice hitting the bottom of my glass, I listen for the melodic tone of e-mail coming into my computer from my real estate agent notifying me of the latest listings. Playfully, I click on each one, staring, studying, and dreaming about the endless possibilities as coffee dribbles from the corners of my mouth. But just as I'm at the pinnacle of my real estate high, my husband walks by, shaking his head and rolling his eyes (which by the way he has become very proficient at over the course of our marriage).

"Why are you doing that? You know we can't afford a new house right now," he admonishes.

"I know. I'm just looking. Some women window shop, I shop for windows."

To avoid argument, I slowly slink away from the computer and head upstairs to put away laundry. I figure this tedious domestic task will take my mind off the beautiful 10-room colonial I had just ogled online. While stuffing socks into an already overflowing drawer, I decide to turn the TV on for a distraction. Was it my fault it happened to be tuned into the *Home and Garden* channel? It took me three hours to put away that laundry, but by golly, I got some great tips on how to turn a plastic milk crate into a stunning nightstand.

I'm trying to turn my attention toward other things. Goodness knows, there are plenty of things that need attention around here.

"Mommy, do you want to draw with me?"

"Sure, honey."

"What do you want to draw?" my son innocently asks.

"Well, how about a fifty year old saltbox colonial with an antique pine door and cascading morning glories on the mailbox and, and…."

Welcome to Mommy Boot Camp

I've always admired our soldiers' bravery and courage and how they selflessly put their lives on the line for our country, but I think their achievement doesn't begin on the battlefield; it actually begins at boot camp. How do I know? I've been attending "Mommy Boot Camp," a.k.a. cardio kickboxing.

At the first class, my friend and I were kindly greeted by the teacher who informed us the first class was free. We were both given a pair of boxing gloves to use, which actually looked more like boxing mittens.

We entered the gym and were instructed by the "regulars" to get two exercise bands and a jump rope. Done! Then we went and stood next to one of the heavy bags placed around the room. Easy enough. We were ready! Or were we?

After a series of gentle stretching exercises, we sensed the mood and the pace was about to accelerate. "OK, pick up your jump rope. Let's start out slow. Get the rhythm. OK, now double time. Let's go—pick up the knees. Faster. Faster. Let's see some sweat." Sweat, are you kidding? My body was like Mt. Vesuvius spewing sweat from every orifice. I watched in embarrassment as these salty masses splat on the mat in front of me. I hadn't sweat like this since I gave birth.

Next, it was on to punching and kicking the heavy bag. "OK,

let's do some jabs. Right hand first. And one, and two. Now add a front kick. Punch and kick and punch and kick. OK, pick it up. You can do it. And five, and four, and three…" Here we go again. I watched the instructor and the women around me, who by the way all seemed to have 0% body fat (only in my dreams), relentlessly pounding the bag as hard as they could. There were women there who were no bigger than my thigh, beating the bag senseless and pushing it clear across the room. It was obvious they were releasing some tension from the fight they had with their husband, kids, boss, or the person who cut them off on the highway. I could almost hear the dialogue going on in their heads.

"If he leaves the toilet seat up one more time, I'm going to…" <BAM>

"I can't believe he told me I was a terrible mother. I'll show him what a terrible mother is. When I get home, he's going to be grounded until he's…." <BAM>

"She wants me to work weekends? What is she, crazy? Why, that little…"<BAM>

These women were mad!

Once the punching bags cried "Uncle", we moved on to the elastic exercise bands. I had seen people use these on the exercise shows while I sat idly by munching on chips and slurping soda, but I had never actually used them. It couldn't be that hard. They were really just oversized rubber bands with handles. "OK, place the handle of the band around your foot, loop it through here, grab it between your legs and begin. One, two, three, four…"

Wait, how do you loop it around your foot? Where do you put your hands? I looked like a floundering fish that morphed into a pretzel. By the time I got untangled, the exercise was over. Phew, that was a workout!

I casually checked my watch and realized the class was only half over. For a minute there, I thought Mickey himself was so exhausted he had stopped ticking. Unfortunately, the clock on the wall confirmed his little gloved hands. I wondered—should I call the paramedics now or wait until the class was over?

After 30 more minutes, the class finally ended. I had survived! I left with a great sense of accomplishment. The only problem—I couldn't walk for two days!

Despite the pain, my friend and I have been back for more classes and are not only getting into shape, but are putting what we've learned to use at home. "OK, eat your cereal, now drink your milk, swallow one, and two. C'mon, pick it up. You can do it. Now get your back pack, run out the door, and catch that bus, in five, four, three...."

Chapter 2
I Can't Help It -- I Was Cracked at Birth

When I was born, the doctor told my mother that I had poor circulation. That definitely explains the sub-zero temperature of my hands and feet twelve months out of the year, but I think it also explains something else—the way my mind works. Sometimes, I don't think the required amount of blood reaches my brain and I see things in a slightly different way than the next person. After reading this chapter, I think you will probably agree that this loss of blood flow is proof positive that I was clearly—Cracked at Birth.

Bar of Soap and a Can of Beans

I'm sort of embarrassed to admit this, but I'm a closet *Little House on the Prairie* fan. So when the "Real Story of Laura Ingalls" was on TV, I was drawn to see what it was all about.

I don't know what it is exactly about this time period that appeals to me. Perhaps it's the simplicity of how life was back then. Now, everything seems so complicated.

In those days, you would get up, wash your face, get dressed, eat the fresh eggs you gathered from the chicken coop, and be on your way. Because there weren't a lot of choices, it was pretty easy to figure out how each day was going to go.

Take a look at today...

You wake up and head for the shower. The good news is—

there's indoor plumbing. The bad news is—you're staring at four bottles of shampoo wondering if you should "volumize, texturize, moisturize or cleanse" your hair today. I don't think Laura had these options. I'm pretty sure she grabbed for the same bar of soap to wash her hair, body, clothes, and the family dog.

As you start to get dressed and reach for your deodorant, you might agonize over whether you should wear the "baby fresh scent, spring garden, or lily of the valley." Back then, the most popular fragrance was probably "Eau De B.O."

Time to go downstairs and have breakfast. Unless you live on a farm and enjoy retrieving freshly laid eggs, you're probably opening your cupboard and looking at 10 boxes of cereal, each box quietly vying for position to be the "chosen" one.

Out the door you go to run some errands. You stop at the gas station and ponder whether to choose, "regular, super, or premium" and pay with "cash, check, credit, or debit." I think Pa Ingalls would have simply grabbed a bale of hay to refuel his mode of transportation. Seems a bit simpler, doesn't it?

Next stop, the 21st century version of the general store—the supermarket. Here you'll find aisles and aisles of "stuff" to ponder over. Should you choose crunchy or smooth peanut butter? Low salt, or all natural? Orange juice with calcium, pulp, no pulp, from concentrate, or featuring a contest to win a free trip to Hawaii? There's toothpaste that brightens, one that whitens, one with stripes, in a pump, in a tube, would you could you on the moon? Could you imagine if Laura Ingalls entered a modern day supermarket? She'd probably have a stroke! And Costco would surely give her a full-blown heart attack.

Well, time for lunch, but should I get a medium, large, or super size it? And, do I want a Coke, Sprite, Orange Crush, or Root Beer? And, would I like an apple pie with that? Ahhhhhhhhhh!

Truthfully, I'm not really sure I would want to live back in those pioneering days. There's something to be said for indoor plumbing and a little heat when you get up in the morning. However, it does make you step back and realize how ridiculous our lives have become. From now on, I'm going to simplify, simplify, simplify. So, if you see me around town pulling into the grocery store on my trusty steed, smelling a little funky—don't stare—I'm only there to pick up a bar of soap and a can of beans and I'll be on my way.

High-Tech Headache

No matter how hard I try, I cannot stay on top of what's the "latest" in technology. I am officially throwing my hands up to the technology gods and admitting defeat.

The sad truth of the matter is that in my business of marketing communications, some think it's imperative to have the latest software, the fastest Internet connection, and the most revved-up PC equipped with mag wheels and chrome bumpers. But, to that I say—Humph!

Maybe I'm from the old school—"if it ain't broke, don't fix it." As a society, we're always trying to make things better, faster, and more powerful than a locomotive. What's wrong with the locomotive if it still gets you where you're going? It may not get you there in 2.3 nanoseconds, but is that really necessary?

To illustrate my point, let's take a look at my computers. I have two pretty fast machines for my business. I try to keep them up to date, but the operating systems seem to change so rapidly, I feel like I'm always a step behind. The problem is, that even if I keep updating my operating system, the programs I use are not updating at the same rate and can malfunction at any time. It's crazy! And, by the time you get everything in sync, it's all changing again anyway. Stop this crazy high-tech train. I want to get off!

Video conferencing is another high-tech novelty I don't think I'll be buying into too quickly. Considering I do a lot of work sitting at the computer in my pajamas with a hairdo that rivals Phyllis Diller, I don't think it would be too good for business.

I did take the broadband plunge, but for the first two months my broadband needed a Band-Aid. After finally convincing my local cable company that it was a bad modem that they supplied, not my computer, I've been whizzing right along.

I've yet to explore MP3 technology. I missed the boat when everyone was downloading free songs from the Web and burning their own CDs, but in my mind, burning a CD sounds dangerous, and one of the software packages to do it is called "Toast." Who wants burnt toast? I'm just a mom with a minivan and a cassette player who can crank *REO Speedwagon* with the best of them.

We still don't have a DVD player since my sons have about 300 videotapes that run on the old VCR. Which brings me to another point—did you ever notice that a lot of high-tech terms are referred to in three letter abbreviations: DVD, MP3, ISP, DSL, WEB? Why is that? Do the developers of this technology think the users aren't smart enough to handle the bigger words? If that were true, then we wouldn't be able to handle the technology either, right?

Cell phones have been suspected of causing cancer and accidents. Whatever happened to rolling down your window and yelling "help" if you're in trouble?

Cable television provides so many channels you can find anything from midget golf to what's playing on Mars. Do we really need to see the latest alien sitcom? We're still on the basic plan at our house: ABC, CBS, NBC, and FOX (there go those three letter abbreviations again).

Truthfully, I wish I could stay on top of technology but realize it would be a full time job to keep up. What I really need after all of this technology talk is a big H-U-G!

Got the Time?

If someone came up to me and said, "Got the time?" I'd say, "Which time, the time on my watch, the VCR, the microwave, or the sundial in the backyard?"

When I get up in the morning and put on my wristwatch, I look down to see Mickey's white-gloved hands pointing at the seven and six, signifying it's 7:30 a.m. I step into the bathroom to brush my teeth and notice the bathroom clock reads 8:30 a.m. It's clear that I haven't changed one of these timepieces for daylight savings—probably in about three years.

I go downstairs to warm my oatmeal and see 7:55 a.m. on the microwave clock. One glance at Mickey, and a 10-minute discrepancy is at issue. While mulling this over, I can hear *Clifford, the Big Red Dog* frolicking with T-bone and Cleo on the TV in the playroom. Experience tells me it must now be around 8:00 a.m. The playroom clock confirms this suspicion stating that it is 8:10 a.m. Still baffled, I use my motherly intuition and send my son out the door to catch the bus when I hear Emily Elizabeth saying it's time for the "Speckle Story." This familiar announcement marks the midpoint of the Clifford show, a.k.a. 8:15 a.m. Besides, who am I to question a big red dog?

I load my other son in the van to go to daycare, and as I start to pull out of the driveway, I glance down at the digital clock on my dashboard. As expected, this time is different than what Mickey is showing. My pulse quickening, blood pressure rising, I decide to put an end to this preposterous punctuality predicament by synchronizing these two timepieces. Unfortunately, the van clock requires me to use a ballpoint pen to depress one button while pushing a second button to change the hour and minutes. Not an easy task while driving. I reflect on the fact that it's funny how this vehicle came with a childproof clock, but the latest news report states that a two-year-old can put this particular model in "drive" and go for an unexpected joy ride. Go figure!

After dropping off my son, I return home and sit down to watch a videotape. I notice the clock on my VCR is blinking and probably has been since the last power outage. I've yet to figure out how to program the VCR, let alone set the clock.

After watching my tape, I go to the kitchen and notice my answering machine is blinking with three new messages. I play them back and think it is odd that they all start off with, "Message received on Sunday at 12:00 a.m." Odd, considering it's Wednesday at 9:35 a.m.

I decide to forget about it and go for a run. I like to time my runs, so I exchange Mickey for my running watch. The watch was displaying the current military time, but by the time I ended my run I was too tired to "do the math." Why this watch had military time, I'll never know. What armed forces would want a 37-year-old mother of two who can't program her VCR and uses a Mickey Mouse watch as her official timepiece?

I really want to put an end to this manic time warp madness. I know there's a phone number that you can call where a voice says, "and the official time is…" Unfortunately, I'm not quite sure what that number is. I tried calling what I thought was the correct number and all I heard was a breathy voice on the other end saying things I can't really print in this column. That's another story for another day. Got the time?

If Only...

If only you could say what's really running through your mind instead of what's politically correct.

So many times I bite my tongue from spewing sarcastic barbs so as not to hurt someone's feelings. But, the witty side of me just wants to slam dunk them with a one-liner. It's a terrible disease, but it certainly is an entertaining sport for a stay-at-home mom who talks in three word sentences all day.

Last week I stopped to rent a video. As I was getting ready to check out, I confirmed with the young gentleman behind the counter that I had a credit from my last rental. He looked at me and said, "Would you like to use the credit for *this* movie?"

Perhaps an innocent question, but what I felt like saying was, "No, I'd like to save all my credits until the end of time and rent out all of the movies in the store. Or, better yet, can I use them toward frequent flyer miles?" Fortunately, my humanity filter kicked in and I simply replied, "Yes, please."

You see, most of us were born with a filter between our brain and mouth so we curb what comes out when we hear something like that. Could you imagine what it would be like if we didn't? I think things would get pretty ugly pretty fast.

This "urge to purge" happened to me again when returning a *Clifford* CD that my son had received for his birthday. It was one we already had, so with sons in tow, I approached the return counter and the young girl working there looked at me, looked at the seal on the CD box, and said, "Are you *sure* you didn't open it?"

Of course I answered graciously, but what I wanted to say was, "Yeah, I opened it, we played the game about 100 times, used the CD as a coaster, ruined it playing catch Frisbee with the dog, and here we are. Oh yeah, and did I mention these aren't my kids, they're just a cover up to make me look like an innocent mother?"

I wish I could stop this runaway sarcastic train running between my ears, but it doesn't seem quite likely. I'm just glad I have the opportunity to share my thoughts with you in this column. Fortunately for me, (and hopefully for you) the filter between my brain and my fingers is at the shop. It needed a good cleaning.

The Reality About Reality TV

{Ring. ring}

"Hello."

"Hi, hon, it's me. Did she pick one yet?"

"Did who pick what?"

"Did the bachelorette pick the guy yet?"

"I don't know."

"Aren't you watching?"

"No."

"Well, what are you doing?"

"Uh, putting the kids to bed."

"Oh. Well, who got picked to go on for *American Idol*?"

"Hon, I don't know."

"Oh, brother. All right, I'm on my way home. I'll find out for myself."

[click].

OK, I admit it. I'm somewhat addicted to *some* of the reality TV shows that are on right now. I emphasize the word *some* because there are a few I really can't tolerate. *Fear Factor*, too gross, *The Mole*, not interested, *Are You Hot?* No. Nor do I care who is, *Married by America*, I don't believe in arranged marriages, and *Joe Millionaire*, well, the guy isn't even a millionaire. Pass.

Still, I do have a few I watch faithfully each week and I'm not afraid to admit it. Why? Because I know I'm not alone. Believe it or not, millions of people tune in each week.

The reality — Although some people might argue these shows are a waste of time, I enjoy them to unwind and quite simply to escape reality. I'd much rather have entertaining chats with my friends about the rise and fall of the bachelors instead of discussing the possibility of another terrorist attack. Quite frankly, I find *reality* quite depressing. Sure, I could huddle in the basement with the kids, a radio, 20 gallons of water, and a stash of canned beans, waiting for what *might* happen. But, if my demise is to occur due to the result of weapons of mass destruction, I prefer to greet God with a smile laughing about the dysfunctional Osbourne's rather than a frightened face created by the dysfunction of Saddam Hussein or some other nut.

My husband has learned to tolerate my obsession, and occasionally I pull him in to this reality TV extravaganza. I realize he's only watching to humor me, plus the fact that I've chained myself to the remote. However, some of my friend's husbands view these shows as pure drivel and refuse to give in to the pleading cries of their wives to watch them. Instead, they demand control of the clicker to watch an intellectual sporting event—like wrestling.

The reality — Whether it's the *Apprentice* or the Celtics, the result is the same. You sit your behind on the couch, crack open a bag of chips, and enjoy a couple of hours of entertainment. What's the difference?

For all of you reality TV junkies, stop hiding behind your

highlighted copy of the *TV Guide* and run into the streets screaming, "I love *Survivor*!"

And, if you happen to be one of the naysayers who have yet
to witness an episode of this new era of television, I challenge you
to just give it a try.

The reality — You might enjoy it.

Birthday Parties Gone Mad

Question: What has happened to kids' birthday parties?

Answer: They've gotten completely insane!

Remember when you were a kid and birthday parties
consisted of Grandma coming over for dinner, Mom serving a
slightly lopsided cake, everyone singing an off key rendition of
Happy Birthday and a few inexpensive trinkets were bestowed
upon the lucky birthday boy or girl? Well, mini-Cirque du Soleil
extravaganzas have since replaced those quaint little parties.

Invitations — No longer is this a casual, "Hey, want to come
to my party?" request. The invitation has become a flashy colorful
direct marketing piece designed to grab your attention so it
doesn't get tossed into the junk mail pile. Upon opening the
invitation, we find that, "this will be the party of the century with
pizza, cake, a juggler, Michael Jordan and more." What child, or
parent for that matter, would want to miss all that?

Location/Entertainment —In the old days, birthday parties
took place at your parents' home, the local park, or perhaps the
church hall. The entertainment consisted of pin-the-tail on the
donkey, dunking for apples, and watching Uncle Norman snore his
way off his folding chair. These days, if the location doesn't cost as
much as your mortgage and you haven't hired a flamethrower,

herd of elephants, or the amazing unicorn, you might as well just skip the party altogether.

Cake — This celebratory morsel has escalated from Mom's sugary concoction to something rivaling a celebrity wedding cake. Generally, theme cakes are the norm, and don't forget a frosting-to-cake ratio of 10:1 for maximum smearage and hyperactivity.

Gifts — In this age of materialism, the last thing our children need is more "stuff." And, the last thing we as parents need is more plastic crammed into a toy box brimming with forgotten toys from birthdays past. But, sadly, so it goes.

Goody Bags — These are the bane of every parent's existence, including yours truly. These sacks of silliness usually cost an average of $8-$10 per child. The contents of the bag generally entertain the child on the ride home from the party, and are then scattered across the playroom floor destined to jam the unsuspecting household vacuum. Since when do you have to give guests attending the party a gift? Didn't happen when I was a kid. Besides, isn't spending time with all your pals enough? And, isn't that what thank you notes are for?

Revolution — I am hereby initiating a revolution to stop the madness. From now on, birthdays should be about celebrating the birth of the child. In fact, I officially started this when I had my younger son's 3rd birthday party. The party was at my home, and instead of hiring expensive entertainment, I called the local fire department and asked them to bring a fire truck to the house. They graciously agreed and I thanked them by offering a donation. And, borrowing from my neighbor's ingenuity, in lieu of gifts I asked everyone to bring a book to be donated to my son's school.

Join the revolution. Don't be afraid. It's up to us parents to stop the madness. It may be hard at first, but with time, you and your vacuum will be off in the corner giving high fives, chanting, "Goody, goody. Goody, goody."

Numerical Nonsense

Did you ever feel like you were just a number wading in a sea of digits? With technology and the fast pace of our lives today, it seems like just about everyone and everything has some sort of numerical value attached to it.

This became quite clear one day as I was out running errands. As I approached the deli counter at the grocery store, instead of someone greeting me by name with a cheery, "Hello, Mrs. Mahoney, what can I get for you today?" I found myself struggling to pull a puny piece of parchment out of an odd looking machine. I waited patiently until a voice from behind the counter acknowledged my presence.

"Number 28?" Makes you feel all warm and fuzzy inside, doesn't it?

After I got home and put away the groceries, I decided to take a trip to the mall. I discovered lots of products are littered with digits, too. I went looking for new sheets and was faced with packaging marked 200-thread count, 250-thread count, 300-thread count, etc. What I wanted to know was, who counts these threads and what exactly do these numbers mean? I think it would make more sense if the sheets were labeled "good enough for company," "only good for camping" and "romance awaits you." Now that tells me something.

Flustered, I decided to make my way over to the children's department, but I couldn't decide if I should buy my son pants that were size 4 or 4T because I really didn't know the difference. So I went to look for some shorts for my other son and stared at sizes 6 and 6X for what seemed like hours. OK, forget about that, I'll go buy something simple—like socks. That should be easy, right? Wrong. Did you know that if you wear between a size 1 and 4 1/2 shoe you should buy socks that are size 4 - 5? Makes perfect sense doesn't it?

I closed my eyes, grabbed a random package, and trudged to the check out line. I handed the socks to the cashier who, never looking in my direction, muttered, "May I have your zip code, please?"

This whole shopping trip was exhausting. I decided I needed a break and called and asked my husband to meet me out for a nice relaxing dinner. As we were sitting there looking over our menus, our waiter approached and asked, "What would you like for dinner this evening, Ma'am?"

"I would like the steak, cooked medium rare, baked potato with butter and sour cream, and the fresh vegetable of the day."

The waiter, staring at me blankly, said, "What number is that?"

I really think this deluge of digits is getting way out of hand. I'm afraid that in the future everything will just be a number. Imagine the conversation around the morning breakfast table.

"Good morning #3, could you pass the #10?"

"Sure, #2. Hey, have you seen my #7?"

"Yeah, it's right where it should be, between the 6 and the 8."

I really can't take this numerical nonsense 1 more minute. This is Writing Chick 01450 signing off on column #41 from her Home 20. 10-4.

Martha Stewart Has Left the Building

One Sunday, after a busy week, I decided I was going to take the afternoon off and do something purely for pleasure—no laundry, no dusting (which isn't a stretch since I never do it anyway), absolutely no housework at all.

So with R&R in mind, I decided to break out my scrapbooking materials that were collecting dust in my closet. For those of you who aren't familiar, scrapbooking is the process of combining photographs, colored papers, stickers, and other artsy crafty stuff in a glorified photo album.

I got involved in this latest craze at the request of my sister-in-law and niece who sell scrapbooking supplies. They asked me to host a party and invite a few friends over to hear their pitch. I was very happy to oblige. Besides, it turned out to be more of a margarita party then anything else, and after an hour or so, the money was flowing freely. As hostess, the more money my friends spent, the more scrapbooking toys I got. So, I kept pouring margarita after margarita. By the end of the night, I felt like I was a contestant on the *Wheel of Fortune.*

"OK Pat, I'll take the trimmer thingy for $30, the rounder doohickey for $15, the stencil thingamabob for $25, the red eye reduction doodad for $10, and the rest on a gift certificate please."

Of course, I had no idea what I had just purchased. I think subliminally, I was hoping the trimmer would give me a hip haircut, the rounder would shape up my backside, and the red eye reduction pen would rid my eyes of that "I'm a mother of two who gets no sleep" look. Unfortunately, this wasn't the case.

Anyway, on this particular Sunday, I decided it was finally time to break out the goods. My plan was to put my columns and some corresponding pictures together as a way of preserving history for my kids. Oh yeah, I also thought it would be a great source of blackmail for those times when they weren't being quite their stellar selves.

So there I sat, staring at this cornucopia of cropping cutters wondering what to do next.

"Mommy, what are you doing?"

"Well, I'm not quite sure," was my honest reply.

"Mommy, what's this?" my curious three year old asked, nearly severing his finger with the mini-paper cutter.

"Don't touch that!"

"WAAAAHHHHHHHHHH!"

"Michael, could you please get these children out of here. Can't you see I'm trying to RELAX?"

My husband, recognizing the familiar sign of a wife-on-the-edge, whisked the children outside.

"Alright, now I can focus. Let's see, I'll use this border, and then I'll put this over here, and this here, and oh no, that doesn't look right. Maybe I should put this here. No, that's not right either. Oh shoot, I didn't want that sticker there. Aargh, I can't get it off." Before I knew it, an hour had passed and I had absolutely nothing to show for it except a splitting headache.

At about the same time, my husband peered around the corner, most likely to make sure I hadn't used one of my fancy cutting tools to slit my wrists, and asked, "Uh, how's it going?"

"Terrible. It's taking forever and it looks awful. I think writing a book would be easier."

"But would it be as much fun?" he sarcastically questioned.

A deathly glare with a pulsing eyeball was about all I could return in his direction.

Bottom line—for some, scrapbooking is very relaxing. For me, scrapbooking is a painful endeavor. I think I'll just keep my memories tucked away in the back of my brain and my photos tucked away in the shoeboxes under my bed. As for my columns, well, I think this little gem will find itself next to my other domestic goddess failures under the appropriate heading, "I'm sorry,

Martha Stewart has left the building."

Weathering the Storm

"Honey, what is he saying about the Nor'easter?" my husband inquired from the kitchen.

"I don't know."

"What do you mean you don't know? You're sitting right there."

"Well, I kind of lost interest after the first three hours!"

Ever since I moved to Massachusetts, I've been amazed at how much they talk about the weather on the newscast when a snowstorm hits. They cover it from every possible angle, and all most of us really want to know is, "Is school cancelled, how long will it take to dig out my car, and will I get fired if I play the ol', 'I tried to get to work, but the roads were too bad' card?"

I grew up in Broome County, New York, otherwise known as Gloom County, or the "other" place the sun don't shine. So, I know all about inclement weather. And, I went to college in Oswego, New York, where it was sport to watch the waifs of the campus get blown around like rag dolls by the lake effect gusts, only to find them later pinned to the nearest chain link fence. The winters were so bad that even the college catalog showed photographs of students hanging onto ropes secured between buildings to find their way across campus. Fortunately, I never encountered that. The only rope I grabbed on those dreadful days was my Soap-On-A-Rope as I headed to the shower and back to bed.

So, after living through all of that, I find these up-to-the-second weather updates a little annoying. I'm sick of hearing, "We're interrupting this regularly scheduled program to give you a weather update." I'll give you an update—the weather stinks!!!

Now let me get back to Jerry Springer and the "Women who hate men and the men who love them."

Despite it all, I can still find the humor in it. For example, my husband and I are fans of two particular local weather forecasters. We tune in to their station when we want the latest weather update. One day when we tuned in, they were mentioning how the station had recently purchased a new weather Doppler. They were so giddy about this new "toy" that they could barely contain themselves. They claimed it was the biggest Doppler in New England, but don't you think that's a little presumptuous? It looks more like a well-endowed snowball on stilts. It's supposed to be so powerful it can determine the weather down to the street level. That's great, but if I want to know what the weather is doing on my street—I'LL LOOK OUT MY WINDOW!

I also find humor in the fact that no matter what the weather, they always find somebody to stick out in the thick of it to help us "feel" how bad it is. I often wonder what this person did to get that detail. "Alright, Smith, this coffee stinks. Now put on your thermals and go stand in the biggest, grayest slush pile you can find on Rte. 93. And, Smith, this time—no boots!!!" I remember one woman they always stationed in the thick of it. Her name was Sally Sanderson. Despite the fact that she had drifts build up along her body from standing outside so long, she seemed pretty happy. In fact, she had a different color knit cap for every storm. Eventually, she retired, and last I heard was still thawing out.

And of course, we can't talk about snowstorms without talking about the Blizzard of '78. Oh my gosh, if I hear about that one more time, I think I'll scream. I didn't live here then, but I heard it was pretty bad. I definitely empathize with the people who struggled through it, but for the love of Pete, it was 27 years ago—get over it!

Besides, nine times out of ten, the storm is never as bad as they predict. In the words of my husband, a life long resident of Massachusetts, "Ah, this storm isn't going to be that bad. It's definitely a fizzlah." (That would be 'fizzler' for those of you not familiar with the language.)

Well, I guess if I'm planning on staying in New England, I'll have to get used to the long-winded weather forecasts and just deal with it. Or, maybe I'll become one of those civilian "weather watchers" who notify the TV station what the weather is like in their town. What the heck, if you can't beat 'em, join 'em, right?

"Hey Sally, got a hat I can borrow?"

Chapter 3
Tales from the Crib

My husband and I were blessed with two cute and very active little boys. Tyler, our eldest, is now nine years old and Andrew is five and a half. They definitely give us a lot of joy, and over the years have done and said things that have given me a lot of fodder to use in my column. I'm hoping some day they will read this book and laugh at the cute and silly things they said and did as a kid. But, I also plan to use these endearing stories as leverage when they hit those rebellious teenage years.

"If you don't clean your room, I'm going to show your girl-friend the story about how you and your brother used to run around and pretend you were *Underwear Man and Diaper Boy*."

Yeah, that should do it.

Hope you enjoy reading about their many adventures and assorted "Tales from the Crib."

Peeping Through the Cat Door

It's 5:30 p.m. on a Wednesday night. Dinner is burning on the stove, my toddler is clinging to my leg like Saran Wrap on an old brick of cheese, and the phone is ringing off the hook. It's just another typical day at the Mahoney household.

As I look out of one eye at my eldest son terrorizing the cat, I'm peering out of the other at the clock wondering when my husband will be getting home to "take me away." Who am I kidding?

The only way I'll be taken away is in a straitjacket as they're hauling me off to the funny farm. And that's on a good day.

Then, alas. Through the din, I hear the "click" of the door opening as my husband walks in. Then, like a well-choreographed dance, I whisk in, hand him the baby, kiss him on the cheek, and gesture à la Fred Flintstone that it's quittin' time and I'm sliding down the dinosaur's back. "Yabba, dabba, doo," echoes throughout the house.

After a long day of being a domestic engineer, I look forward to the opportunity to have some "mommy time." This particular night I decide that going down to the basement to lift weights and do a few laps on the treadmill is just what I need to unwind.

For a moment, it's quiet. I feel like I may have actually escaped. For the first time all day, there are no kids clinging to me, yelling for me, hunting me down. I grab my first barbell of the night and then IT happens. I feel like I'm being watched. Am I just being paranoid? I look around and there is clearly no one else in the basement besides a few cobwebs and me. Then, I look up. At the top of the stairs I see two little blue eyes peeping at me through the cat door. I leap over the cat litter so as not to be spotted, but to no avail. The next thing I hear is this little high-pitched voice saying, "Hi Mommy." Say it isn't so. Soon, there are two pairs of eyes glaring at me as if peering at a caged tiger. If only they knew.

It wasn't long before a third pair of eyes could be seen looking at me. This bigger and wiser set of peepers seemed to understand the glare of a mommy who needed to be alone and a wife that would be very difficult to live with if all of these eyes didn't disappear—QUICKLY!

Could somebody please tell me why, when a mother leaves a room, she's all of a sudden on *America's Most Wanted* list of hardened criminals and is being tracked down by her offspring and the family cat? I guess this phenomenon is akin to the one that has designated our telephone a child magnet whenever it is within an arm's length of mommy's ear. And, it must be a not-so-distant relative of the one that doesn't allow you to spend more than 15 minutes at a restaurant to enjoy your meal.

The funny part is, I actually cherish all of these phenomena. If it weren't for the adorable little creatures that created them, I wouldn't have the pleasure of writing this column.

Mommy, Who's God?

With the holidays and the recent Osama Bin Laden controversy, religion has been at the forefront of a lot of people's minds. It's definitely made me think more about it and how important it is to raise our children with some sort of religious foundation. The only question I'm struggling with at the moment is, at what ages do kids actually "get it?"

My five-year-old has been going to church off and on since he was born. Admittedly, we don't get there every Sunday, but we do our best. Even if we don't make it to church, my husband and I try to talk about God and religion when we're outside the "big white building." I think right now, his innocent perspective is that God created people, animals, trees, plants, and all the things that make up a little boy's imagination. Sometimes, I think he understands more than that. When he was four, he surprised me by saying, "Mommy, didn't God give us a beautiful day?"

Proudly, I replied, "Why yes, honey, He certainly did." It makes me think that perhaps his appreciation of God is blossoming just as his youth.

Of course, this recent understanding is a new thing. When he was three, he accompanied my husband and me to Sunday service. We stood to sing a hymn and happened to notice a fly buzzing about. As if in slow motion, we watched as our son methodically grabbed a Bible from the back of the pew, whacked the fly, watched it fall to its death, and returned the Bible to its original position. My husband leaned over and whispered, "His work is done." Sure, it was humorous, but I realized he had not yet grasped the concept, "Thou shalt not kill."

Then there was the time we were at church and I glanced down and saw him practicing his Picasso on the back of the pew. Mortified, I removed the pencil from his hand and told him he would have to clean that up after church. As we started to wipe away the "evidence," I noticed the paint on the pew was coming with it. I grabbed his hand, whisked him out of church, and realized my actions just erased the lesson of "doing the right thing." His artful rendition remains there today as a reminder of this failed lesson.

Maybe five is the magic age of "enlightenment." Recently, after Sunday school, I asked him what he had learned. He clearly said, "I learned that Jesus is the Son of God." Great, I thought, he's finally getting it. The next day as we sat at the breakfast table, sun streaming in the window, I overheard him mutter, "Oh, Jesus." After explaining to him that we don't say the Lord's name in vain, he innocently replied, "But Mommy, he's in my eyes." It then dawned on me that Jesus had just become the "sun" of God.

Nevertheless, we continue to take our boys to church and try to teach them the meaning of religion and doing the right thing. Hopefully at some point they'll truly "get it." Until then, I guess I'll just enjoy the innocent comments out of the mouths of babes and answer their questions the best I can. When they ask, "Who is God?" I'll answer. When they ask, "Where does God live?" I'll answer. When they ask, "Where do babies come from?" I'll answer, "Go ask your father."

Underwear Man and Diaper Boy Rule the World

Every night after dinner as the sun begins to set, two super-heroes suddenly appear in my living room. They aren't your typical superheroes that dominate the airwaves or the toy aisles, but none other than Underwear Man and Diaper Boy. There they stand with their hands on their hips, bellies protruding, and ready to conquer all evil.

I'm not quite sure how Underwear Man and Diaper Boy originally came on the scene, but I imagine it was one innocent evening when we were trying to get the two superheroes ready for bed and started undressing them downstairs. Big mistake. Now, it doesn't matter who's at the house at that "magical hour." Friend or foe, these two capeless superheroes streak around the house for whoever is in their path.

Both of them have learned from watching the masters. Diaper Boy is currently taking cues from his mentor, Batman (also referred to as simply, "Man.") In fact, Batman is so special he made it into our family photo. There he sits clenched in the palm of my white-knuckled two-year-old. It made my son so happy to have his buddy in the picture, until Mommy conveniently cropped him out when putting the picture in a frame. This attempt to annihilate his superhero was greeted with a voice quivering, "Wherrrrrrre's Maaaaaaaaan?"

Sometimes I wonder if Batman is enjoying all of this atten-tion. I must say, he's quite a trouper. He's had his feet dragged through a soggy bowl of Cheerios, he's suffered the embarrassment of wearing Mr. Potato Head's hat, he's been swimming in the toi-let with his arch enemies, and he has even made it through a rough and tumble hour of play at the McDonald's playground. At one point, we almost lost him to the ball pit. I had visions of me diving headfirst into this colorful kaleidoscope and starring in the next superhero episode, *Mother of Man, Swallowed by the Sea of Orbs.*

Imagine if we adults decided to unleash our superhero identities in the darkness of the night? Unfortunately, I think if Underwear Woman and Boxer Man suddenly appeared on our neighborhood streets, so would the police with a couple sets of handcuffs.

I know at some point, Underwear Man and Diaper Boy will have to stop making appearances, but for now, we're going to let these little superheroes rule the world. Goodness knows somebody's got to do it.

Yoga — Don't Try This at Home

Recently, my six year old son came home from school and said, "Mom, guess what?"

"What?" I said with sincere curiosity hoping he wasn't going to tell me he flushed the class mouse down the toilet—again.

"We did yoga today," he declared proudly.

"That's great honey. Show me what you learned." I watched as he moved his body in positions any contortionist's mother would be proud of.

"This is the downward-facing dog, the child's pose, the plank, and oh yeah, the cobra."

"That's great, honey. Want to do Mommy's yoga tape with me?"

"OK," he said with glee.

Yoga has been around for years, but I had no interest in

trying it until my sister said, "Kath, just try it. I swear every time I finish my yoga class I feel like I've just gotten a massage." Well, that was good enough for me. I'm a sucker for a good massage. Now I was excited to embark on this activity with my son hoping for a special mother-son bonding experience.

I popped in my favorite tape, *A.M. Yoga for Beginners* with Rodney Yee. I first heard about this tape on *Oprah* and it became my favorite because it was filmed on a sandy beach, the poses are relaxing, and quite frankly Rodney Yee is nice to look at in his Speedo at anytime of the day.

My son and I started off fine and were enjoying the serene music and the soothing sound of the ocean hitting the rocks. Then, as I was on all fours in cat pose, POUNCE! My three-year old jumped on my back and started yelling, "Giddyup, Mommy," slamming his heels into my sides. How's that for a mother-son bonding experience? After removing him and nursing a couple of bruised ribs I caught up to Rodney again. Then, while lying on my back in relaxation pose drifting off—OOMPF! "Hi, Mommy." My three-year old had just assumed the full bouncing diaper pose right in the middle of my stomach. Not quite the kind of massage I was looking for.

Nevertheless, I continued to do Rodney's tape from time-to-time (sans kids) and I even tried to step it up a notch and do some yoga that promised an aerobic workout as well. I figured, great, I could get a massage AND burn some calories. Good in theory, but it went more like this…

"OK, downward-facing dog to cat to cow to plank and HOLD. Now, thread-the-needle go into the tabletop and grab your ankle and put it behind your head." Ahhhhhhhhhhhhhh! This was no longer a massage—it was torture! And, to make matters worse, I was performing this contortion in my living room in front of a picture window that looks out onto our street. I can only imagine what the average passer-by was thinking. "Hello 911. Uh, yeah, I just passed my neighbor's house and I think you better send an ambulance. It looks like she's having a seizure." I ended up shutting the tape off and assuming the reclining chair pose.

I'm not entirely ready to give up yoga, but I think there should be a couple of additional warning labels on the video boxes. "WARNING: Performing yoga with children under five within a 100-mile radius can be hazardous to your health. Trained professionals should perform advanced poses ONLY. If you are a novice, you will probably find these tapes soothing to watch, but please, don't try this at home."

He's Not My Kid

"I want my Mommmmeeee," my 3 1/2 year old screamed from the front of our church. The minister was just about to deliver the children's sermon and all of a sudden my son realized his lifeline wasn't with him. Acting on mother's intuition, and the desire to avoid further humiliation, I tossed my hymnal, ran to the front of the church, scooped up my son, and sat down. Gee, do you think anybody noticed? Well, yeah, the entire congregation to be exact.

This behavior was something new for my son. He has always been a pretty easy-going child, but for some reason, church brings out the worst in him.

The following week, trying to avoid another outburst, I took him up to the front of the church myself for the children's sermon. Did it work? No. This time, he decided he didn't want to sit in the front pew; he wanted to sit in the side pew. Why? Who knows? I'm sure it was just another strategic move in his diabolical plot to force me into living a life in dark glasses, wig, and oversized chapeau.

When we returned to our seats, I prayed the worst was over. I figured, if anything, it was a good place for a prayer to be answered.

Then, the usher came by to offer us bread (body of Christ) for communion. I took a piece and handed it to my son since it was his first time receiving communion. Before I could instruct him what to do with it, he shoved it in his mouth and grabbed a fistful more off the plate, practically wrestling the usher to the ground. I must admit it was rather amusing at the time until I looked up and saw the minister's eyes staring back at me. I quickly found out that there was indeed enough room under the pew for a 5'8" woman to hide.

When the usher bravely came back with the grape juice (blood of Christ), this time my son followed my instruction and waited before he drank. But, before the sigh of relief even left my body, he picked up two empty juice glasses and put them up to his eyes and shouted, "Ahoy, matey."

It's a known fact that kids were put on this planet to shamelessly embarrass their parents. Heck, we did it to our parents so now it's payback time, right? But, do they have to perform these antics in the most inappropriate places. Well—yes they do!

I think all parents can attest that at times they would rather not claim ownership to the toddler screaming and thrashing about on the floor at Toys-R-Us. Some, including yours truly, might have even slinked away and stood amongst the crowd watching this freak of nature, pointing, and shaking their head saying, "He's not my kid."

Sometimes, they are at least nice enough to limit the

embarrassment to just a few friends versus an entire public establishment. Here's an example. One time we went to visit my friend and she happened to comment on how tall my eldest son was getting. Feeling proud as a peacock, he stood tall and using me as a yardstick reported, "Yeah, see—I'm as tall as Mommy's penis." Fortunately, this was my college roommate who had seen me naked and was quite certain I didn't have this anatomical feature. Nevertheless, my face was as red as an overripe tomato.

I understand this embarrassment is all "part of the territory," but what my children don't know is that I'm secretly plotting my *revenge*. Turn the clock forward ten years. My sons and their friends are hanging out in our basement and in walks Mom, a.k.a. me, wearing a fluffy pink terrycloth robe, elephant slippers, curlers, green cake makeup, and for an added touch, a little black wax on my teeth. I can see their mortified little faces right now as they try to slink out of the house and explain to their friends, "She's not my mom!"

Run, Puppies, Run

Every year my kids are home for winter vacation and soon after, a week of spring vacation. I'm never quite sure what to expect during these little breaks or what to plan. I don't know if my boys will be on their best behavior or if their heads will be spinning like the evil Regan from the *Exorcist*. Regardless, I do know one thing. No matter what, every day I need to "let my puppies run."

Winter break is especially tough. It's usually too cold and snowy to just open the door and let them out. I tried to spend some quality time with them inside, but it didn't take long before they were scratching at the front door, pining to be free. So what's a mother to do? I took the puppies to a huge indoor gym resembling a McDonald's playground on steroids.

The day we went, it happened to be "Carnival Day." In other words, cha-ching! Talk about grabbing a parent by the Kibbles 'n Bits. They had me right where they wanted me and I had to cough up the cash or endure the pain and embarrassment of leaving the place with two little nipping puppies attached to my ankles. I plunked down the money and secretly hoped the woman behind the counter would hand me a couple Valium with my receipt, but no such luck. So, off we went.

What was so special about Carnival Day? It was an opportunity for the puppies to run on both sides of the building (versus the usual single side), ensuring their parents would never find them again. The place was so big it was virtually impossible to track your child's every move. You almost needed to set up an invisible fence around the perimeter and attach an electronic shock collar to your child to make sure they didn't exit the premises. But, somehow, I don't think that would go over well with the Department of Social Services.

Then it began. Hundreds of puppies were chasing each other in every direction. The littlest ones were getting kicked around like an empty dog dish.

"Watch out." CRASH!

"Bombs away." CRASH!

"Here I come." CRASH!

"Ruff crowd," I heard one of the little ones mutter.

Then there were the parents. Some were thrilled just to be sitting. Some were attempting to read, but I doubt they were actually reading. The noise in there pierced your skull like the high-pitched sound of a Chihuahua howling at the moon. I found this out when trying to make calls on my cell phone.

"Hello, Sue." <silence>

"Sue, are you there?" <more silence>

I couldn't hear a thing on the other end, but I'm pretty certain whomever I was calling got a good dose of heavy panting. To those of you I tried to call that day, I apologize, except for my husband, he likes the heavy panting.

Oh, and can we talk about the germs? For every runny puppy nose, there was a puppy coughing up a lung, and another one sneezing a spray that could put out a five-alarm fire. The littlest puppies were slobbering all over the balls in the ball pit and I prayed some puppy didn't lose their lunch (or worse) anywhere in the place. I tried not to think about it and just sat there quietly, 20 packs of anti-bacterial wipes at the ready.

After about an hour and a half, my puppies were ready for a nice juicy bone and an afternoon nap. Me too. So, home we went. Since they were able to get their daily dose of tail chasing, the rest of the day went pretty smoothly.

I'm not sure what spring vacation will bring. I'm hoping the weather will be warm and the puppies can go outside every day and run to their heart's content. Of course, if we're doomed with April showers and stuck inside again, I can guarantee that all naughty little puppies will be heading straight for the doghouse.

Chapter 4
Not My Mother's Daughter

My mother wears pressed slacks; I wear wrinkled sweatpants with random paint stains. My mother's house can easily pass the white glove test; I save dust bunnies to use as snowy backdrops for my Christmas decorations. My mother says, "fiddlesticks" when she's upset; I say things that would make a sailor blush. Despite it all, we're great friends, but sometimes I think I'm—*not my mother's daughter.*

I think many of you will definitely be able to identify with the columns in this chapter, no matter what your relationship is with your mom. One way or another, our mothers are an integral part of our lives and help shape us into the people we are today.

The title of this chapter is based on the name of one of my most popular columns. I received a lot of e-mail from women who could definitely "relate." I hope you can, too.

Not My Mother's Daughter

I love my mother. She's my best friend. But sometimes I wonder if we're really related.

My mother is the consummate housekeeper. She could have given Barbara Billingsley a run for her money in the casting call for June Cleaver. Growing up, you could eat off her kitchen floor, we always had creases running down the center of our pants, cookies and milk were waiting for us when we got off the bus, and family dinner was ready promptly at 6:00 p.m.

Turn the clock forward 30 years and here I am as a wife and mother. My house often finds itself on the Richter scale as a class five earthquake, I could use the dust bunnies in the corners of my living room to make sweaters for the kids, and some nights, dinner consists of something that looks vaguely familiar retrieved from the bowels of the refrigerator.

Is it a sign of the times? Is it the fast-paced world we live in? Or, is it just that we are indeed very different? My mom claims that in her day, having an immaculate home and well-kept kids were what women aspired to. As a woman of the 21st century, I aspire to make sure I pick up my son from daycare, get my other son to soccer practice, make the 5:00 p.m. FedEx pickup, and get us all home in one piece. As far as priorities go, housework is down there with cleaning out the cat box.

Yup, we're definitely different and my mother doesn't hesitate to point out these differences. Each time she visits, it's only a matter of time before she says, "You know what you need is…." Now, the first few years, I'd listen intently. Mother knows best, right? Now, I still listen intently, but I ponder the advice before accepting it. One year I "needed" a glass butter dish. I wasn't aware I "needed" a glass butter dish. Does the butter taste better in a glass butter dish? The next visit, glass butter dish in hand, my mom informed me, I "needed" a teakettle. Hmm! My husband and I don't drink tea. Is it a requirement to have a teakettle sitting on the burner of your stove? If it is, why didn't they sell us one with the stove?

Besides differing views on domestic issues, my mom and I have different views about fashion. I've never been one to care too much about appearances, but when my mom goes to the mall, it's not just a shopping trip, it's an event to dress for. She puts on her nice slacks (a mom word), a nice blouse (another mom word) and her best lipstick. I grab the closest sweatpants, a shirt without baby drool, and smear on some ChapStick.

Of course, if you ask my mom, she'll deny the fact that she really cares about what others think. Then I remind her of the time we were in a public place and my brother raised his voice to confront her on the issue and she responded, "Shhh! Someone might hear you." Case closed!

Despite our differences, I love my mother dearly and look forward to her making the six-hour trek from upstate New York to visit. In fact, I really wish she lived closer. I have a teakettle that needs dusting.

Motherisms

Did you ever listen to yourself and think that your mother was in the room with you? You know, repeating the phrases she said that drove you crazy when you were a kid?

For instance...

In the winter, my mom would bundle me up for school in about 20 layers of clothes as if I were dressing for the Iditarod sled dog race. First, there would be the long underwear, pants, turtleneck, and wool sweater that itched like crazy. Next would come the blue snorkel coat with the fake fur lining around the hood, and string pulled so tightly all you could see were my eyes, and all I could see was the fringe of the fur hanging over my brow, swaying back and forth in cadence with my muffled breathing.

Next, my mother would put on my wool mittens, scarf, and carefully place my feet in plastic bread bags before putting on my snowmobile boots. I'm still not sure what the bread bags were for and why I had snowmobile boots when we didn't own a snowmobile, I haven't a clue.

Anyway, as I stood there in the kitchen looking and sounding like Darth Vader, I'd complain about how ridiculous I looked. She would smile sweetly and say, "You'll be warm as toast." Maybe that's where the bread bags came into play, but when you're a pre-pubescent teen, you want to look "cool," not like a piece of crusty old bread. Man, I hated that expression. So what do I say to my son before I send him out in his green puffy coat and his knitted wool scarf that wraps around him seven times? "You'll be warm as toast." It has to be in the DNA.

My mom had other sayings she used when she wanted to motivate me to excel in whatever I was involved in. She would use the typical expressions that we've all heard— "Practice makes perfect" and "Where there's a will, there's a way." Of course, as an adult, sometimes you don't realize that you're even using these "motherisms" because they've become so second nature. I didn't realize it until one day when I heard my son talking to himself in the other room. I peeked in to see what was going on, and as he was struggling to shove his little brother into the toy chest he was muttering, "Where there's a will, there's a way." After I pulled my two year old to safety, I looked in the mirror and declared, "Oh my gosh, I've become my mother."

I guess it's an expected course. I'm sure my mother got some of those expressions from her mother, who got them from her mother, and so on and so forth. I decided that it's an inevitable path, so I might as well have fun with it. "C'mon kids, clean up your toys. He who maketh the mess, cleaneth the mess. C'mon, quick as a bunny. Honey, did you finish your lunch? Waste not want not. Did you know children are starving in China? C'mon, I'm not getting any younger."

Oh, my poor children.

Quick! Call the Grammar Police

I love writing, but I must admit, it hasn't always been my passion. In the past, it was a chore to get my thoughts down on paper and grammar was something I always struggled with, and still do. Fortunately, I have a mother who graduated from the reputable Katharine Gibbs secretarial school, a well-read sister, and an editor who are all there to catch my grammatical gaffs before they get printed.

I'm not sure when this disdain for grammar first began, but I think it was sometime in middle school. My report card would come home for my mother and father to sign, and my mother would come up to me and say, "You know, your grammar really needs help."

My reply, "Why, is she sick?"

I think there were just too many rules to follow and I've always been a little rebellious. You know, like, "i" before "e" except after "c" and something about how much does your neighbor weigh. Quite frankly, I think that's a bit personal.

My mother was constantly on my case (and still is) when I said, "bring" instead of "take." What's the big deal as long as *it* gets to where *it's* supposed to go?

It didn't help that the rules of the written word have changed. How do I know this? I attended a grammar seminar while working at my last job. The instructor was at the front of the class telling us that there are no longer two spaces after a period—now there's just one. As I picked my jaw up off the floor, I thought to myself, "They can't do that. The rules of grammar are like the doctrine of the Catholic religion. They can't be changed. Has someone called the grammar police to report this?" I never could remember the old rules, and now they're changing them? I'm doomed.

Then along comes e-mail, and another set of rules rears its ugly head. For instance, you're not supposed to write your messages in capital letters because the reader may interpret that as yelling. Come on now, if I really wanted to yell at somebody, I'd pick up the phone and give them an earful.

And don't forget about those cute abbreviations. You know the ones, like "lol" for "laugh out loud" and "<g>" for "giggle" and my least favorite, the annoying smiley face :).

Teenagers have their own set of code to keep us parents from knowing what's going on. Did you know "POS" means "parent-over-shoulder?" And, here I thought these kids were having intelligent business conversations about the "point-of-sale."

I think I'll always struggle with grammar; it's just one of those things. However, I'm not going to let it stop me from achieving my dream of writing a book (see, you're reading it right now). Lucky for me, when we were going through the final editing stages, the grammar police were at the local donut shop.

Just a WYSIWYG Kind of Gal

The older I get the less I feel compelled to pretend to be somebody I'm not. You know, like cleaning my house with a bulldozer and sandblaster before company comes to make them "think" I'm an immaculate housekeeper. Not going to do it.

Gone are the days of putting on makeup to go to the mailbox! From now on, borrowing the computer industry term for user-friendly software, I'm going to be a WYSIWYG kind of gal: *What You See Is What You Get.*

I'm sure this new attitude will make my mother cringe, but that's all part of it, not worrying about what anybody else thinks. It's not like when you're in high school when image is everything.

Heck, back then I wouldn't leave the house unless I was wearing the hottest GUESS? jeans and coordinating IZOD shirt (I do believe I had one in every color.) Those days are long gone.

If you think about it, who am I trying to impress? And why? I've located and landed my husband; my kids tell me I'm beautiful despite my disheveled morning hair, streaked mascara, and adult acne breakouts; I conduct most of my business via phone or e-mail so none of my clients actually see me; and most of my friends have known me long enough to realize—J. Lo I'm not. So, why put on the big show?

A friend of mine, on the other hand, hasn't "seen the light" just yet. I'm trying to educate her on the beauty of this WYSIWYG type of life, but I think I've got my work cut out for me. She still feels the need to please, impress, and strive toward perfection—whatever that is. I must admit, she always looks great, her kids look great, and her house is virtually spotless. However, even she admits that trying to achieve this level of flawlessness is an exhausting endeavor. When I asked her about it, she said, "I know. I wish I wasn't this way, but I can't help myself. I mean—what will people think?" Sounds just like my mother.

Recognizing the stress this young mother of two was under, I suggested she hire my cleaning service so at least she wouldn't feel the need to clean the house *just in case* the UPS guy stops by. Her response, "I couldn't do that. I'd have to clean the house before the cleaning people got here so they wouldn't think I was a slob." Like I said, I have my work cut out for me.

These impeccable imposters are everywhere. Why, just the other morning, I spotted a woman who I assumed was a stay-at-home mom standing in the produce aisle at the grocery store. There she was with her Gucci handbag, Ann Taylor ensemble, perfectly painted nails, and two immaculately dressed small children in tow. I followed her around the store like a stalker waiting for her to show signs that her life couldn't possibly be as flawless as it appeared. Up and down the aisles we went, and nothing. "Come on," I thought to myself, "Be realistic. Underneath that $300 sweater you're just like the rest of us—a stressed out mother on the verge of a nervous breakdown with body parts hanging down to the same ankles left battered and bruised by too many Tonka truck collisions." Then it happened. Just as she was bending over to grab her low-fat yogurt, the infant she was holding tossed his organic cookies all over her shoulder. Quickly, I wheeled my cart into the next aisle and performed a silent victory dance. I knew it. She *was* one of us.

From now on—*what you see is what you get*—a slightly overweight, non-Martha Stewart, tomboy crazed mother-of-two who writes a column about everyday life to maintain her sanity. This admittance of my authentic self might be shocking to some, but hopefully empowering to others. To them I say, let down your hair, kick off your heels and enjoy being, well—YOU!

Chapter 5
Home Is Where the Chaos Is

In general, my husband and I are very happy homeowners. When we bought our house in 1995, we were thrilled. We would be moving from a four-room apartment near Boston where you could literally vacuum all four rooms from one outlet, to a four-bedroom house in the country. To us, this house was a mansion.

After awhile though, things that you once thought were "cute" or "chic" become "disgusting" and "irritating." The faux marbleized vanity counters in our bathrooms and the particle-board cabinets in our kitchen went from "trendy" to "trash" in a very short time.

Anyway, every home has a story to tell, and these are some of ours.

I Just Gave Birth to a Kitchen

We're having our house renovated, and I've decided that the process is like having a baby.

Deciding to conceive: It all started last year. We had just visited my sister and saw their beautiful new house. As we drove home, I looked at my husband and said, "We need a new house."

My husband, used to my spontaneous thought process and knowing that agreeing is the best defense, said, "OK." That was it. My foot wasn't even out of the car door before I was lunging for the Real Estate section of the newspaper.

After thumbing through the paper for nearly an hour, realizing that a new house in our area costs more than NASA's entire space program, we decided that perhaps it would be best to renovate. We still had to ask ourselves, "Will we be able to afford it? Are we ready emotionally? Do we want to settle down here?" After answering, "Yes" to all of these questions, we decided to take the plunge.

Conception: The first phase of the process was the "trying" part. Trying to find someone to design our new look and trying to find a contractor to build it. Fortunately, one of our neighbors gave us the information we were looking for, and soon the blueprints were drawn, the contracts signed and (sparing the intimate details) the plan to renovate was finally conceived.

First trimester: At first, my husband and I were glowing with anticipation. We studied the plans and talked about what life would be like "post-renovation." But it still didn't seem real. We were hesitant to tell our friends and family right away until we were absolutely sure. Twelve weeks later, our contractor arrived on our doorstep, hammered his first nail, and our dream was now a reality. It's a moment I'll never forget.

Second trimester: Although the amount of time it took to do our renovations was considerably shorter than an actual pregnancy, it seemed like forever. It was only two weeks into the process and I was already feeling uncomfortable. We had to set up camp in our dining room and the discomfort and inconvenience of everything being covered with dust, eating peanut butter and jelly for virtually every meal, and doing dishes in the bathtub were almost more than I could bear. We knew there was something beautiful coming at the end of this ordeal, but each day as I brushed sawdust out of my hair, I thought to myself, "Never again."

Third trimester: OK, by this time I'm pretty much miserable. The kids and I have now been prisoners in our living room (a.k.a. our dining room, playroom, and TV room) for the last four weeks. Security gates keep us contained to our "area" and keep my baby from catching the wrong end of a power saw.

My 5-year-old is now hysterical each time the hydraulic nail gun goes off and I find myself muttering, "I can't wait for this to be over."

The birth: The dust has settled, the lights have been hung, the wood floors glisten and it's almost time for the "big moment." With sweat dripping off the contractor's brow as he puts on the finishing touches, we tremble with anticipation. It's time. We turn on the lights, see the glow of our new Corian countertops, and are overwhelmed with emotion. Tears roll down our cheeks as my husband and I look at each other and declare, "It's beautiful." My husband then turns to me, hugs me sweetly, and asks, "Want to do the basement next?"

Of Mice and Woman

"What is that smell?" I questioned with crinkled nose pointing skyward.

"What smell?" my odoriferous-challenged husband replied.

"That smell."

"I'm sorry, honey, I don't know what you're talking about."

"Over here. It seems to be either on the rug or coming out of the air-return vent."

"I still don't smell anything, honey. Sorry."

"Oh, brother."

Lucky for me (or not), I was born with a fairly large odor detector, a.k.a. schnoz, and it detected a putrid smell in our dining room. My husband, on the other hand, was blessed with eyesight rivaling our nation's bird, but his sense of smell is pretty much non-existent. For me, the stench was unbearable. Every time I sat down to eat, whatever I ate tasted like that—that—*smell*. And even when I left the room, this nasty scent seemed to jump aboard the interior of my nostrils and follow me everywhere. It was driving me crazy. What the heck was it? Then it dawned on me.

"Honey, remember that scratching sound you heard in the wall a couple of days ago?" I inquired.

"Yeah."

"And remember that baby mouse I saw running through the hall that made me scream like a school girl?

"Yeah."

"Well, I think Junior's parents met their demise between the 2 x 4's holding up our wall."

"Gross. So now what?"

"I don't know. You're the man of the house—do something."

I'm not exactly what you would call a timid woman and would normally have taken charge of the situation myself, but I draw the line at seeking out dead rodents. Like a trouper, my husband went to the basement to see if he could unearth anything below the stinky wall.

After a brief inspection that seemed like a Mighty Mouse millisecond, he emerged to report, "Didn't see anything. Sorry."

"OK, Lenny," I thought to myself, referring to the mouse-loving giant from Steinbeck's classic, *Of Mice and Men*.

It was obvious we didn't have the same concern about the matter, especially when he responded, "I'm sure the smell will go away soon. Just forget about it."

Forget about it? Who is he kidding? He's been married to me long enough to realize I'm not one to just *forget about it.* God bless Mickey, but I wasn't about to share living space with his ancestors. And where were our two felines? I had a few words for them. They've managed to kill virtually every four-legged creature scampering through our yard and leave it on our front steps, but somehow these little varmints eluded their capture. What's up with that?

First order of business—research. I scoured the Internet asking Jeeves and anyone else who would listen, "How do you get rid of dead mouse smell in your wall?" The all too frequent answer—wait!

WAIT! I can't wait. There must be some product out there to solve the problem. You know, like *Mouse-be-gone* or *Odor-go-bye-bye*? Nope. Nothing. According to the information I found, the only thing you can do, outside of taking a sledgehammer to your wall, is wait until the creature 'dries out' and stops emitting the putrid smell. Great, just great.

So what have I learned from this experience? I won't be renting the movie *Willard* anytime soon, our cats are freeloaders, my husband would never make it as a perfume-fragrance tester, I won't be inviting the neighbors over for a dinner party, and the saddest realization of all: a tiny, insignificant, furry little creature has defeated me. Mouse—1, Woman—0.

Homeland Security

I think President Bush's Homeland Security initiative is a great step toward keeping America safe from those who want to disrupt "the land that we love." In fact, I think it's such a great idea, I decided to institute a little homeland security in our own home.

Home Security System — Right now, I like to say we live in a gated community, so it's pretty safe. There are gates at the bottom of the stairs, at the top of the stairs, in all the bathroom doorways, and other strategic places throughout the house.

If anyone ever entered our home uninvited, they would either have to be a rocket-scientist to operate the gates or a world-class hurdler to get over them. If neither was true and they decided to "take the leap" anyway, I think once they left, they would be pretty easy for the police to spot. They would be the ones roaming the streets with a strange gait, speaking in an octave rivaling that of the late Hervé Villechaize a.k.a. Tattoo from *Fantasy Island.*

Telecommunication Security — My next line of defense is to rid our phone lines of those troublesome intruders, better known as telemarketers. Prior to the "do not call registry," I received between five and ten calls a day from somebody trying to sell me vinyl siding, a new roof, a windshield for my car, or a free trip to Hawaii just for visiting a timeshare in Kalamazoo, Michigan. Since I put our phone number on the registry, you would think the number of calls would be reduced significantly. WRONG! Now, I get the same number of calls from non-profit institutions.

Don't get me wrong, I understand these individuals are just doing their job and my husband and I are happy to donate money, but not via phone during our dinner hour when I have two kids wrapped around my ankles.

So, I decided to conduct a survey among friends and family on the best way to respond to these calls to politely let them know, "We're not able to offer a donation at this time, but thank you for calling." Below are what I thought were the best responses.

"Hello, is Mr. or Mrs. Mahoney there?"

"I'm sorry, this is the nanny. The best time to reach the Mahoney's is between 7:45 and 7:47 p.m. every other Tuesday, except if there's a full moon, and then they won't speak to anyone. Why don't you give me your home phone number and I'd be happy to have them call you back? Now, what time do you eat dinner?" (Click).

Or, this response my mother told me my very religious deceased aunt used to use—and seriously meant it.

"Hi, is this Mrs. Mahoney?"

"Yes, it is."

"We're collecting donations for the "free the ants" campaign and we're going to be stopping in your neighborhood over the next few days. When would be the best time for us to stop by?"

"Oh, anytime is fine. Who will be coming? I can't wait. I have so much to tell them about the Lord, Jesus Christ!" (Click).

There, that should do it.

I'm still working on solutions for keeping junk mail, unsolicited e-mails, and door-to-door salespeople at bay, but I'm having a little trouble. The first two shouldn't be too difficult, but I don't think I'll ever have the heart to tell little Suzy down the street that I just don't *need* 12 boxes of Tagalongs or Do-si-do's.

Welcome to Command Central

Did you ever notice that with the beginning of school, so begins the chaos of trying to juggle everyone's schedules? There are sport practices and music lessons for the kids, PTA meetings, volunteering, and occasional workouts for the parents, and a host of other things. It's a scheduling nightmare.

To that, I would like to introduce (drum roll please), "Command Central."

Command Central is my answer to all of your scheduling skirmishes. It consists of a large blackboard with the days of the week written across the top. Under each heading are the planned activities for the day. This schedule is changed every Sunday night, by yours truly, for the upcoming week.

Attached to the blackboard are two calendar pages displaying the current month and the following month. This is called the "Master Schedule." It contains all of our doctor's appointments, karate lessons, reminders to order sediment filters for the water softener, and other important information.

Some may call Command Central anal-retentive, but I prefer to think of it as "organizational genius." It works very well—at least for me. My husband hasn't fallen in love with it just yet and isn't quite sure how it works.

The other day he yelled from the living room, "Honey, I've got a golf tournament this Sunday." Quickly I scurry to the kitchen to confer with "the schedule."

"Are you sure, honey? It's not on the calendar."

"Yeah. I know I mentioned it."

"Sorry, you know the rule, if it's not on the calendar, it doesn't exist." After a little grumbling, he concedes. Of course, once in awhile, to keep our marriage intact, I have to succumb to a "non-scheduled" activity. It's painful, but after all, I vowed for better or for worse.

Now I'm working on my eldest son. The other day he asked, "Mommy, can Billy come over to play tomorrow?"

I grabbed his little hand, marched him over to the blackboard, grasped my pointer and said, "Well, honey, if you look here, first you have school, then after that, we need to get the oil changed, then you have karate, then we meet Daddy at the gym so Mommy can play basketball, and then Daddy will take you home, feed you, bathe you, and put you to bed. So, I guess the answer is 'No,' OK?" The glazed over look on his face was enough to tell me this lesson did not compute.

Oh well, I'm not going to let them get me down. I still think organization is key to running a well-oiled household. Remember about a decade ago when they came out with that computer, "Audrey," allowing you to post everyone's schedules, keep track of phone messages, answer e-mail, and do a bunch of other cool stuff? I thought I had died and gone to heaven. I couldn't wait to get my hands on one. Unfortunately, it wasn't in the budget at the time and then Audrey just disappeared. Whatever happened to her? Now I just defer to my own Audrey, my mother, and yes, her name is actually Audrey. She's pretty good at helping me fill in the blanks on the Master Schedule, especially people's birthdays.

"Don't forget, it's Julie's birthday on Friday," she informs me.

"Who's Julie?"

"You know, your third cousin, twice removed, on your father's side? Don't forget to put it on your calendar."

"OK, thanks Mom." I'm glad someone understands the importance of "the system."

In time, I'm sure the rest of my family will realize how Command Central keeps things running smoothly in our household. Who knows, they may even start writing things down on their own.

Hmmm. I wonder when I should tell them about the back-up schedule on my computer?

Chapter 6
I Love You Honey, But...

I have been married to my wonderful husband, Michael, for 14 years. Our secret to a happy marriage is rather than criticizing each other's foibles, we just laugh at them. Neither of us is perfect and we know it.

Unfortunately for my husband, I have a platform to share his idiosyncrasies with the world. And, although sometimes I don't think he's too happy about that, he puts up with it hoping that some day I'll become a rich and famous author and he can laugh all the way to the bank. We can only hope.

The Purger Meets the Hoarder

In this corner, Patty the Perilous Purger asserts her position as a woman who believes—if you haven't used something in the last ten minutes, it's outta here.

And, in this corner, Harry the Horrendous Hoarder, who believes—there is no such thing as clutter, but rather a collection of worldly possessions that should be cherished and honored until the end of time.

"Honey, what are you doing?" my husband questions.

"I'm purging all of your…your…junk."

"What do you mean, junk?" my husband incredulously demands as he holds up a 3-foot Seagram's bottle he "acquired" in college and uses to hold pennies. "You can't get rid of this, it's…it's…history."

The taunting has been going on for awhile, leading up to this final drag out match. He hoards, I threaten to purge. Now it was time for Patty to send Harry to the mat in a major body slam.

The bottom line is, my husband can't throw anything away. He has jeans and sweatshirts with holes larger than Clinton's story about his involvement with Monica Lewinski. I've tried to replace these abominable articles, but when I ask him why he continues to wear them, he looks at me and says, "They're comfortable."

My reply, "Well, so is a muumuu, but you don't see me wearing one of those around the neighborhood, do you?"

I don't mean to be hard on the poor guy; I just don't understand this squirrel mentality. Maybe it's because he came from a family of eight children and there wasn't much you could call your own. I'm really not sure. On the other hand, I know exactly why I like to purge. I'm a visual person and if there is stuff lying around that isn't pleasing to the eye—it's outta here.

My husband's hoarding rears its ugly head in our office as well. Because this is where I conduct my business, I've only allowed him one desk drawer for his "stuff." One day, he called from work and asked me to get something out of his assigned drawer. I was happy to oblige, but when I tried to open it, it was like trying to pry a pair of leather pants off a not-so-slender individual on a hot day. When I finally managed to wedge it open, I was mortified at what I saw. When I confronted him, his reply, "I was going to get to it."

"Why would you want to 'get to' six years of old pay stubs, three years of old magazines, and a fuzzy green potato chip?" was my response. I decided I'd "get to it" first. It all went in a box and into his closet, sans potato chip.

News flash—my eldest is showing signs of this hoarding behavior. He loves to make arts and crafts and cannot seem to part with any of them. I don't want to be heartless and throw them away, but on the other hand, I don't want to wade through a sea of paper dinosaurs for the next decade either. I'm hoping he outgrows it, but if not…

Patty the Perilous might be in the ring once more to defend her title. Stay tuned!

One Big Scaredy Cat

My son and husband have just embarked on a new adventure together. They have become part of the Boy Scouts of America. More specifically, my son has become a Tiger Cub and my husband is the Tiger Cub leader. When they first announced the news, I was truly happy that they had found something they could bond over. Or, maybe it was just a sense of relief that this was something I didn't have to be involved with. As a mother who is constantly driving her kids to all sorts of activities, not being involved in one of them would be a nice break—or so I thought.

"Hello, honey."

"Yeah?"

"The highway is a parking lot. I don't know if I'm going to make it home in time to run the Tiger Cub meeting. You might have to get things started."

"You're kidding, right?"

"No, I'm serious. The traffic isn't moving. I don't know if I'm going to make it."

As I felt the color drain from my face, I quickly threw down the phone, and sprang into action: the act of sweating, shaking, and running though the house like a crazed animal. After all, what did I know about Tiger Cubs? I heard my husband and son talk a little bit about it, and knew it entailed dens and packs, but I didn't really comprehend the whole thing. I mean, to me, a den is a room where you watch TV and a pack is something women travel in when they go to the bathroom. It was official; I was having a panic attack.

"OK, get a grip," I said to myself. Let's see, the other night I watched as my husband practiced making tiger snouts and snakes out of paper plates, it couldn't be that hard. I also knew he had plans to decorate their flag—but how—and with what? The stress was mounting. I didn't even know what the Tiger Cub motto was. Was it, *"Truth, Justice, and the American Way?"* No, that was Superman. I was doomed.

I decided the best defense is a good offense, so I started doing some research. According to the information I found on the Boy Scouts of America Web site, I learned that being a Tiger Cub is the first level of Cub Scouts. After that, the boys become Bobcats, Wolves, Bears, and Webelos. What the heck is a Webelo? Was this some breed of animal that I had just never heard of? Upon further research, I learned that WEBELOS is actually an acronym for "**We**'ll **Be LO**yal **S**couts." Mystery solved, but it didn't tell me anything about making tiger snouts, and it was almost time for the meeting to start. Aargh!

About 6:15 p.m., my husband called and said, "Honey, I'm almost home. I think I'm going to make it."

As quickly as the color had left my face, it came back. I stopped sweating, grabbed my younger son, put him in the car, and stood in wait like a mother tigress ready to pounce on her prey. At 6:20 p.m. my husband pulled in the driveway, and at 6:21, we pulled out. We were headed to the neighbor's house to feast on pizza with another mother tiger and her two cubs. Ahhhh, now I could relax, and you know what? It felt GRRRRRRREAT!

The Defining Role

The other day, my husband handed me a sweater and said, "Can you hand wash this for me, please?"

After I stopped laughing hysterically, I looked at him and said, "Sure, let me pull out my washboard and find a nice rock in the sun to dry it on." Slightly annoyed, he dropped the sweater on my side of the dresser where it still sits. It's been two weeks.

I find it interesting how men and women decide in their minds what role each of them should play. For instance, why did my husband ask me to hand wash his sweater? Was it because I do the other laundry, because it's "women's work," or because he doesn't know how? Clearly I'm no authority on hand washing. I can't remember the last time I hand washed anything, much to my mother's dismay. When I was working in corporate America she used to call me on Sundays and ask, "Are you washing out your pantyhose for the week?" After all, isn't that what all working-women did on Sunday nights?

And, every Sunday I told her the same thing, "No Mom. I haven't worn a dress or pantyhose to work in three years." After a frustrated sigh, she usually changed the subject.

Of course, I must say, I do the same role projection on my husband. For instance, if I have something that needs to go down to the basement, I'll put it by the basement door for him to take down. I can't really explain why I don't walk it down myself. It's not like I'm afraid of the looming darkness or that I'm lazy. It's just, well, because the basement is the "man's domain."

When we first got married, this role defining was difficult.

You want to make sure everything is "fair," but let's face it, nobody wants to get stuck cleaning the toilets. It becomes a big negotiation and over time, things have just sort of evolved. Now we have it all worked out. He feeds the cats, I feed the kids, he loads the dishwasher, I rearrange the dishwasher, he buys the food, and I eat the food.

It's a great system, even though I did get stuck with cleaning the toilets. But you know what? Heidi's Cleaning Service does an excellent job.

How to Make Your Husband Leave the Room in 10 Seconds

Recently, I rented the movie, *How to Lose a Guy in 10 Days*, starring Matthew McConaughey and Kate Hudson. I must say, I was pleasantly surprised. It was very funny.

In the movie, Kate Hudson is a "how to" writer for a woman's magazine, and after hearing about several dating disasters from her female co-worker, she decided to write an article proving these dating faux pas would make any man run for the hills. Of course, like any reputable writer, she needed to prove her theory. Kate chose Matthew McConaughey as the object of her "rejection" and implemented ruthless tactics she was sure would drive him out of her life if not out of his mind. Without giving away the whole movie, suffice it to say her methods were hilarious.

After watching the movie, I got to thinking, "Hmmm, is there a column idea here?" And in similar bizarre voices-in-your-head fashion, I responded, "Definitely."

First, let me clarify that by no means do I ever want to *lose my guy*, a.k.a. my husband, at any point in this lifetime. But, I thought, there are those times when I wouldn't mind a little *alone time* and might want him to vacate the room temporarily. So, I started thinking about things I could say or do to accomplish this. And, like any reputable writer, I needed to do research.

My first tactic was to engage him in conversation. My husband isn't much of a talker, so this alone makes him squirm. So, over a period of days, I decided to try out a few lines I was pretty sure would make him disappear faster than Houdini. These are the ones that seemed to work the best:

"Honey, I want to adopt a baby—maybe twins."

"Can you rub my feet?"

"Can we talk?"

"Did I tell you my mother is coming to stay with us for three weeks?"

"What do you think of these floral curtains?"

"Do you know what was on *Oprah* today?"

"Do you know what Dr. Phil said about husbands like you?"

"Did you see the list I left of things that need to get done around here?"

"Can you buy me some tampons while you're out?"

"Want to watch *The Young and the Restless* with me?"

"The cat threw up in the basement. Can you clean it up?"

"Do you want to go to the ballet?"

"I think the next car you buy should be a minivan."

"Did you call the doctor about getting a vasectomy?"

"I think I'll cut my toenails now."

"Want to do this yoga tape with me?"

"I'm having a Mary Kay party here in 15 minutes, but you can stay if you want to."

"What do you think about painting our bedroom pink?"

"Honey, do you think this is a wart?"

"Cable's out. Wanna cuddle?"

But the one phrase that made my husband leave the room at break-neck speed was when I asked…

"Honey, do I look fat?"

Attack of the Lawn Grubs

Ah, it's a beautiful, sunny spring morning. As I open the door to take a long awaited breath of fresh spring air, I am suddenly overwhelmed with…

(Cough, cough, cough), "Oh, man. What is that smell?"

Upon closer inspection, I am able to detect the cause of this odoriferous offender perpetrating my airways. I had seen it before. With the melting of the snow and the first blossoms of spring peeking through the hard, cold ground, the men in the neighborhood were out in full force spreading the contents of their freshly opened bag of Scotts Lawn Pro Step 1 on the flat brown canvas in front of them. Their blank stares were reminiscent of a scene ripped from the movie, *The Stepford Wives*, but appeared to be from the soon-to-be released sequel, *The Stepford Husbands, Attack of the Lawn Grubs*.

I don't know what happens to men this time of year, but it's always the same. It starts with the analysis of each blade of grass, each grub-ridden patch, each mole hole. It's as if they're studying the competition, preparing for the big game.

When we first moved here ten years ago, we were novices at lawn care. We didn't know crabgrass from crab cakes. All we knew is that we had a lawn that looked like the latest convention of bad toupees, and things haven't changed much since. When I tried to take action by calling 1-800-GET-LAWN, my husband grabbed the receiver from my hand and in that same robotic fashion I had just witnessed, groaned, "No, honey, I'll take care of it."

Off he went to Home Depot with the other Stepford husbands. They walked the aisles until they spotted their good friend Scott. As they bowed to him they droned in unison, "I need GrubEx, Weed Control, Crabgrass Preventer…"

They had their arsenal. They were ready for battle.

The next morning they were outside in full force, spreading their secret weapons all over their lawns. As the kids and I huddled inside, my son asked, "Mommy, what is Daddy doing and why does he look so funny?"

"It's OK, honey. Daddy is just trying to make our lawn look pretty."

"Well, when can we go out and play?"

"Not until you're 18."

Unfortunately, Daddy's master plan didn't work. I can't fault him, though. What is a man raised in the streets of Boston supposed to know about grass? Back then, it was something you smoked, not something you mowed.

Now that spring has officially sprung once again, that familiar glint in my husband's eye is back. It really kind of gives me the creeps. Just the other night when I asked him, "Honey, what kind of grub do you want for dinner?"

His reply, "Grub bad. Me kill grub."

Help! I'm afraid, so very afraid.

Selective Listening—Nature or Nurture?

I always accuse my husband of selective listening when it comes to our conversations. It's a constant battle for someone like me who makes a living communicating. In fact, it bugs the heck out of me.

"Honey, I got a lot done on my book today."

"Book? What book?"

"You know, the one I've been talking about for the past two years?"

"Oh, yeah. What's it about again?"

"A collection of my columns. I can't believe you have to ask that. Haven't you been listening?"

"What?"

And so it goes. Sadly, I see this trait trickling down to my eldest son. He's a great listener when it comes to what's on television or memorizing the lyrics of songs. He never misses a beat. In fact, it's a little bit frightening.

For instance, one morning when I was watching the *Today Show*, a commercial for a birth control product called Ortho Evra came on. Tyler and his little brother were sitting next to me and I was hoping they weren't paying any attention. No such luck.

"Mommy, you should get that," my eldest exuberantly recommended.

"No, I don't really need it."

"Why not?"

"Well, I just don't need it."

"But it stays stuck on you."

"Yeah, for seven whole days," my youngest piped in.

Both of them would be great salesmen. They can tell you all about the benefits of every product that crosses the screen.

Dexatrim — A weight loss supplement

Knowing I would like to use a few pounds my son offered, "Mommy, maybe you should get that. It takes off pounds instantly." Gee thanks.

HoverDisc — A large inflatable flying toy

"Mommy, can you call and order the HoverDisc? It's totally safe and you can use it again and again. And, it doesn't take batteries. Here's the number. I can't call 'cause you have to be 18 years or older to order."

Braid-O-Matic — Allows you to braid your own hair.

"Mom, you should get that. It makes perfect braids every time." Obviously, not only does he not listen to me, but he also fails to notice I have short hair that would be virtually impossible to braid.

One time I was researching a car using the Web site Vehix.com and my son entered the room. Just by looking at the computer screen he recognized the logo and said, "Oh, Vehix.com, your road map to the automotive world." I told you it was frightening.

It's not just TV he's listening to so intently, it's anything that interests him. Two years ago we went to see Disney on Ice, and even in the chaos my son focused in on a man standing on a podium selling programs for the show, yelling out his sales pitch. With all of the activity going on around us, I barely knew he was there. But my son's selective hearing tuned right in and said, "I think we should get one of those."

"What?"

"One of those," he said pointing to the program the man was holding.

"Why?"

"So we'll remember this day for years to come."

Does that sound like the natural commentary of a five year old?

So, why is it that the teacher's voice and my voice are like annoying background noise?

"So Tyler, what did you learn about today?"

"I dunno."

"Who did you play with?"

"I forget."

"Did you buy milk for lunch?"

"What?"

More often than not I feel like Charlie Brown's teacher whose mouth moves but all the kids (and husband) hear is, "Wah, wah, wah, wah, wah, wah." It's so annoying! So, to get my husband or kids to do anything, I think I'm going to have to start talking in 30-second sound bites.

For my husband…

"And you too, can finish your basement all by yourself. Just call 1-800-do-it-now for more information. Just think about how proud you'll feel when it's all finished."

And for the kids…

"Want to look like a superhero? Just drink your milk every day. It's fortified with all of the essential vitamins and minerals you'll need to save the world."

Or, how about this…

"Yes, you too can enter the contest, *"I have the cleanest bedroom in America."* Just send us a photo of your spotless room and you could win a totally safe inflatable HoverDisc. Send it now and we'll throw in the super Braid-O-Matic. It makes perfect braids every time."

Yeah, that should do it. Wish me luck!

The Four-Wheelin' Fool

Last year my husband bought a pick-up truck. Unbeknownst to me, he always wanted one, so I gave him the thumbs up to purchase the vehicle of his dreams. That was my first mistake. Since then, I have watched my street-smart city boy husband transform into a backwoods four-wheelin' fool.

When he first got the truck, it was winter and he couldn't wait to try out the four-wheel drive. Of course, neither of us practical car drivers could figure out how it worked.

"I think you push that button and pull the stick shift this way," I suggested.

"No, that's not right," he proclaimed as the truck jerked and bucked. "Just get the manual out and read it to me." I'm really not a manual type of gal, but the thought of us being thrown through the windshield wasn't too appealing either. So I read, he shifted, and an obsession was born.

"Where are you going?" I questioned wearily one night.

"Out."

"Out where? It's 11:30 at night and it's snowing."

"Yeah, I know," he said with a grin from ear-to-ear. "I want to take the truck four-wheelin' on the dirt road."

"Are you kidding? Go to bed."

My breath was wasted; he was already out the door and down the driveway. This went on for awhile, but when spring came, suddenly he changed his focus to wanting to haul stuff. It didn't matter what stuff, he just wanted to haul it. Every weekend he was hauling something to the dump, whether it needed to go or not.

"Hey, where are you going with my dining room table?"

"To the dump."

"Get back here." That was the end of that.

But he couldn't stand seeing the back of his truck empty. Now he was almost encouraging me to buy large appliances and furniture just so he could go pick them up. I kept telling him, "But honey, you don't need to pick them up, the store will deliver them."

"Nonsense. We have a truck now. We aren't paying delivery charges anymore."

"But delivery is free."

Once again, my breath was wasted; he was off and running. Since then, he's picked up a washing machine, a patio set, and a mattress.

Of course, in order to pick stuff up, you need something to tie it down with, right? According to my husband, ropes are for rookies. This is where I learned about the world of "truck accessories."

"Honey, I need bungee cords to keep stuff from falling off the truck."

"OK," figuring safety comes first.

But it didn't stop there.

"Honey, I need straps to keep stuff from falling off the truck."

"But you just got bungee cords."

"I know, but that's for the smaller stuff. I need straps for the bigger stuff."

"All right. Whatever."

Once again, things *seemed* to settle down, until…

"Honey, I need a cover for the back of the truck."

"Why?"

"To keep the snow and rain out and to make it more aerodynamic," he explained with glee.

"Whatever. Do you realize this truck has more accessories than Elton John?"

And then summer came, and a new line of accessories was suddenly in demand.

"Honey, I need a rack on the back of the truck so we can carry a canoe without scraping the top of the cab."

"But we don't have a canoe."

"But we might get one."

"Well, gee, you might as well put on a hitch to tow the boat we don't have yet either."

"Good point."

"Don't you think you're getting a little carried away? Next thing you know you'll have a gun rack and a wad of chewing tobacco in your mouth."

"No I won't," he said quietly as he spit some dark gooey substance off to the side.

Well, I've had about enough of this. Little does he know, next year I'm planning on buying a new vehicle and I know exactly what I'm going to buy.

"Honey, where did you get that motorcycle?"

"Well, you said we needed to replace the minivan."

"Yeah, but a motorcycle? Where are the kids going to sit? And where are the kids anyway?"

"Oh, they're at your mother's house. The side car comes next week."

A Horse Off Course

The other day my husband went for a run at the oh-dark-hundred hour of 6:30 a.m. Personally, I'm barely conscious at this time of day, but he seems to be wide-awake and rarin' to go. He took his usual scenic jog down a country road where traffic is sparse, especially at this hour. He said he was making good time until, on his return trip, he spotted a horse walking toward him. It was just a horse, no human attached. It was definitely a horse off course.

Being a humanitarian, as well as a past equestrian, my husband couldn't just let the horse walk around aimlessly so he stopped and asked, "What are you doing out here by yourself Mr. Horse?" Surprisingly (well maybe not), there was no reply. "All right, c'mon. Let's see if we can find your owner." My husband grabbed the reins of his newfound friend and started walking with him in the direction the horse had come from.

"This is crazy. Where the heck do you live?" Once again, no reply. Instead, the horse spotted some weeds and stopped to have a little snack. Now this was really throwing off my husband's running time and he wasn't too pleased. "C'mon buddy, we gotta find out where you live." So, the horse finished his snack, lifted his head, and started walking back to the road. He tried to take another detour but my husband, forever the cautious one, pointed out, "You can't go down there, you'll get hurt."

"OK," said Mr. Ed (just kidding). They continued their journey.

Afraid he would have to go door-to-door, my husband remembered a home where he had seen a horse in the past. Could it be? He walked up to the gate at the end of the driveway, but it appeared to be locked, so he tried to lead the horse through a narrow opening to the side of the gate. The horse must have had width-o-phobia because he didn't want to go through there and wasn't going to budge. Getting a little agitated, my husband scolded, "C'mon, I think this is where you live." Nothing. "Oh man, like I need this." My husband decided to try the gate again. Fortunately, it opened, and they walked through.

Now, you must realize that my husband still wasn't sure if this was where the horse lived, but he walked the horse up to the side door and knocked on it anyway. At this point, it was still very early—about 7:00 a.m. Can you imagine if you lived there and opened the door to find a strange, sweaty man holding the reins of a horse? Or better yet, if you were having your morning coffee and you witnessed all of this nonsense out the window? Personally, I would have thrown on the deadbolt and dove for the phone to dial 911. Unfortunately, we'll never know how the real homeowners responded because no one answered. What a shocker.

My husband didn't know what to do next, so he started to walk toward their garage that appeared to be converted into a stable. It had horsy paraphernalia inside as well as an ample supply of hay. He led the horse toward the garage and the horse headed straight for the hay. My husband took this to mean, "Ah, home sweet home." I took it to mean, "Man, am I hungry. Get the heck out of my way."

We're still not sure if that was the horse's home, but if it wasn't, I would have loved to have seen the faces of the people when they woke up and found him in their garage.

"Vern, what's that?"

"Where?"

"In our garage."

"It's a horse!"

"But we sold our horse last week."

"Well, I guess he's back."

It's a tale about a horse off course they may never know—well, at least until now!

Chapter 7
Holidazed & Confused

What can you say about the holidays? They are supposed to be a time when family and friends get together to celebrate, enjoy lots of food and drink, and be merry. Unfortunately, for me, holidays bring one more thing—STRESS. I don't care how you slice it, the holidays are stressful. So much to do, so little time, and too many darn people in the mall keeping you from doing it. Sure, all the lights may be lit and the stockings hung with care, but instead of, "'Tis the season to be jolly," it's more like, "Get the heck out of my way or you'll be sorry!"

Going forward, I'm going to try to focus on the joy of the holidays, but in years past, they went something like this...

Sounds of Christmas

"I want dat."

"Me, too."

"I want dat."

"Me, too."

'Tis the season for toy manufacturers to flood the airwaves with commercials about the hottest toys on the market, and how no kid should be without them. Faster than a 30-second sound bite, our 3 1/2 year old son falls hook, line and sinker for these pitches, drooling over every colored piece of plastic flashing before him. My eldest son, equally mesmerized, validates the drool-worthiness of each toy by giving his approval. It's these sounds that remind me Christmas is right around the corner.

However, despite the number of "I want dat's," echoing from the playroom, when put on the spot, neither of my children can come up with a single item for their Christmas list. It's as if Scrooge has swooped in and erased their memories of commercials past.

"OK guys, let's make your list for Santa. What would you like for Christmas this year?"

"I dunno."

"C'mon, think about all of the things you've seen on TV. What were they?"

"I dunno."

"Alright, well here are some catalogs (seven to be exact). Let's go through them and we'll circle the things you might like."

"OK."

Of course, I have already told them Santa will only be bringing three gifts this year just like baby Jesus received when he was born. Amazingly, they bought into this without a struggle, but only after I named the 20 friends, family, and relatives that will also be giving them gifts. I could tell that making this "limit" had an effect on my older and wiser son's selection process. He knew if he only got three gifts, they had to be *good*.

"How about the Yu-Gi-Oh trading cards you wanted?"

"Nah, I'll buy those with my piggy bank money."

"How about that karate headband you asked for?"

"No, I don't want it anymore."

"How about a scooter?"

"No."

"Mini-trampoline?"

"No."

On one hand, I was quite pleased he wasn't being greedy, but on the other hand, I had siblings and grandparents breathing down my neck to send them a Christmas list. I started to break out in a sweat and suggested anything and everything just to get something down on paper.

"How about a new bike?"

"No."

"An automatic go-kart?'

"No."

"A 50 foot blow-up Tyrannosaurus Rex?"

"No."

"A 70 inch plasma TV with surround sound, SONY PlayStation 2 with 300 megahertz processor, and all of the latest DVDs?"

"Huh?"

My youngest son was of no help as he crawled all over the back of the couch, not paying any attention to what we were doing.

"What about you, Drew? What would you like for Christmas?"

"I'm a monkey," he shouted with glee.

For a second there, I thought maybe we wouldn't need to buy

into all of the commercialism that surrounds Christmas. After all, my husband and I always make a point of explaining the true spirit of the holiday and I think my oldest son has a pretty good appreciation for what it's all about. But realistically, I was a kid once and I remember how exciting it was to open presents on Christmas morning. I could only imagine the tears if there was nothing under the tree this year except fallen needles, dust bunnies, and my cat swatting at the Mickey Mouse ornament. So, I decided to defer to my husband.

"Honey, the boys aren't giving me any ideas for gifts this year. Do you have any thoughts?"

"I dunno."

Great. It was clear I was on my own on this one.

"Wanna watch TV?" my husband asked.

"Sure."

(click)

"I want dat."

"Me, too."

Merry Christmas, Leon

Recently, my husband and I offered to write something for our church's Advent Devotional booklet and were asked to come up with some family traditions that brought back fond memories. It wasn't as easy as it may sound.

Mike went first. His fondest memory was lighting the Advent candles with his family. Each year the kids took turns lighting the candles from eldest to youngest. Since there were eight kids, Mike's youngest sister had to wait patiently before it was finally her turn.

His father always read a scripture from the Bible and it was a special time for their family.

Then, it was my turn. Sadly, I think as a kid, I was too immersed in thoughts of Santa and the unwrapping of presents to truly appreciate the real meaning of Christmas. That, and having a terrible memory, I knew this wasn't going to be easy. At first, my most vivid memory was helping my mother decorate the house for the holidays. I enjoyed taking the decorations out of the attic and carefully placing them in their "Christmas spot," especially these four decorated boxes that we put on the mantle each year that spelled out N-O-E-L. I used to love to rearrange them so they spelled L-E-O-N just to drive my mother crazy. It was funny at the time, but I wasn't sure if it was a story that I wanted to share with our church.

So, I kept thinking. The memory I ended up sharing was that of setting up the nativity scene each year. I enjoyed taking the figurines out of the crinkled tissue paper and placing them carefully in the stable. In retrospect, it was quite a spiritual feeling to finally place baby Jesus in the manger next to Mary and truly realize what Christmas was all about. Of course, by the end of Christmas day, the animals were usually somewhere on Old McDonald's farm and the wise men were driving around with Barbie in her convertible.

Now that our kids are old enough to grasp the true meaning of Christmas, we're trying to develop our own family traditions. So far, we've decorated our house, sans LEON, and taken our annual trip to cut down our Christmas tree. My husband has hung the lights outside and (thankfully) removed the blinking ones that we mistakenly bought a few years ago. They made our house look like a used car dealership and explains why people kept pulling into our driveway and kicking the tires on our minivan. He also took great care in minimizing the number of lights so it didn't look like the "house that threw up Christmas."

Beyond the decorations, we are also doing things to concentrate on the spiritual side of the holiday. We have hung our Advent calendar, we're going to make gifts for some of the cousins, and we're taking toys to a homeless shelter. Hopefully, with all of this, my kids will realize that Christmas is about giving and celebrating the birth of Jesus.

Yep. It's a great season, and I really enjoy spending time with family and friends at all of the holiday gatherings. I wish all of you a very safe and happy holiday season, and if you happen to see Leon, please tell him I said, "Merry Christmas."

Next Christmas I'll...

Well, we had a wonderful Christmas this year and hope that all of you enjoyed your holiday. Everything went off without a hitch except for the foot of snow that kept us from going to Grandma's house Christmas afternoon. We decided the snow was pretty to look at but wouldn't be pretty if we were turned around backward in our minivan on the highway.

However, even though everything went rather smoothly, each year I inevitably find things I would like to do differently for the coming year. I usually make a list of these things, put it in a safe place, and hope I remember where I put it when Christmas rolls around the following year. In the spirit of David Letterman, here is my top ten list of things to do differently for next Christmas.

#10 – Play the "Santa card" more often to keep the kids under control while out shopping. "Honey, please stop pulling the price tags off the clothes. Remember, Santa knows if you've been bad or good, so be good for goodness sake." I think I'll try using this reminder throughout the year since apparently, mommy doesn't have the same clout as the big bearded guy.

#9 - Purchase baker's pastry ruler (if there is such a thing) when attempting to make mother's cinnamon bun recipe. Somehow, I don't think using my husband's tape measure is the proper way to measure dough when you're baking.

#8 – Don't spend an exorbitant amount of money on gifts for the kids when they end up making a fort out of cardboard boxes and destroying it with the $10 last-minute toy you bought them.

#7 – Buy separate "Santa" wrapping paper so the kids don't say, "Mommy, why do all the presents Santa left look just like the ones you wrapped for Grandma and Grandpa?"

#6 – Check to make sure there are no Snuggle dryer sheets stuck in clothing before walking down the aisle in church Christmas Eve to avoid embarrassment of having one fall out the bottom of your pant leg.

#5 – Buy more than one Christmas CD so Johnny Mathis doesn't sound like Porky Pig by the time Christmas rolls around, "Si – si – si – si – I say – Silent Night, folks."

#4 – Measure length of Christmas tree and cut appropriately BEFORE erecting in the middle of the living room and scraping the plaster off of the ceiling.

#3 – Make sure toys come with assembly instructions in English or don't require assembly at all.

#2 – Defrost Christmas Eve cornish game hens a little earlier to avoid having to wake husband at 11:00 p.m. to tell him, "Dinner's ready."

And the number one thing to remember for next year…

#1 – Kindly hint to husband that you really don't wear brooches and giving you three of them is definitely *way* too generous.

Now, on to my top ten New Year's Resolutions I probably won't keep.

Walking Around in a Holi-daze

Since January 2nd, I've been shuffling around the house in my white fluffy slippers with a glazed look in my eyes. I'm not quite sure why, but I just can't seem to snap out of it. I think I have post-traumatic holi-daze.

I've never suffered from this before, but when I find myself walking into the living room to plug in the long gone Christmas tree lights and plug in the cat's tail instead, I know something's wrong. I guess I'm saddened by the fact that Santa's sleigh has flown back into the cardboard box he calls home the other 11 months of the year, the stockings are no longer hung with care, and I no longer see the back of the UPS deliveryman running from my front door after leaving package after package. I miss Brown.

And, even though most signs of Christmas are gone, I can't seem to part with all things Christmas. My CD player is still loaded with my favorite Christmas music, lights still adorn the front of our house, and the brown wreath on our front door still hangs proudly, despite the fact that it's losing needles faster than Britney Spears dropped her first husband.

I'm sure I'll snap out of this sooner or later, but it doesn't help that I've already blown three out of the five New Year's resolutions I set. Maybe I can start over on the first day of the Chinese New Year. That'll buy me about a week and a few pints of Ben and Jerry's.

In the meantime, I'm trying to get my kids to set some resolutions. After explaining to them what they were, I said to my eldest son on a recent trip to McDonald's, "Honey, I've got a New Year's resolution for you."

"Yeah, what is it?"

"I think you should be more positive and try and look at

things in life as half full." Perhaps I was subliminally thinking about myself based on my current funk.

"What does that mean?"

"Well, if I were holding a glass of water (motioning to an imaginary glass in my hand) and the water went up to here (pointing to the center of my imaginary glass), would you say the glass was half empty or half full?"

"Neither. We're not allowed to have glasses in the car."

"I know, but if we were, what would you say?"

"Half empty."

"Why is that?"

"'Cause Andrew probably drank the other half."

"Did not."

"Did too."

I decided to try the conversation with my younger son. I looked in the rearview mirror to get his attention, but when I was greeted with an index finger plunging deep north up his nostril, I decided to drop the subject. Based on that visual, I also decided to drop lunch that day.

Well, I actually think writing this has helped me pick my chin up off the floor a little (only a plastic surgeon can pick up the other one). Perhaps the haze of the daze is lifting. I decided to share my excitement with my husband.

"Honey, you know how we always come up with a corny rhyme to ring in the New Year? Like last year, we joked, 'It's all about me in 2003.' I'm trying to think of one for this year. Wanna help?"

"Sure. How about, 'Out the door in 2004.'"

Gulp! The daze continues.

Can't You Just Feel the Love?

With the lights down low, candles glowing, music playing softly, it was the perfect atmosphere for a romantic Valentine's dinner, until—"Uh, honey, it's me. I'm going to be late."

"What do you mean you're going to be late? It's Valentine's Day."

"I know, I know, but we're in the middle of this big project and it just blew up." My husband started sharing the technical details of this debilitating dilemma, but the words were lost on me. I just watched as the wax dripped off the candles and pooled on my nicely pressed tablecloth.

Suddenly, the sound of my son's voice snapped me back to reality. "Hey, Mommy, will you play dinosaurs with us?" my son eagerly inquired. "You can be the T-Rex." At this point, that sounded like a good idea since I felt like ripping somebody's head off. "Wow, Mommy, you really look mean. You're a good T-Rex."

Well, at least something good came out of this mess. After a few more shrieking roars and limb dismemberments off the swarm of plastic dinosaurs that surrounded me, I decided I would stick to the original plan of getting the boys to bed by 7:30 p.m. when a local caterer was supposed to be delivering our romantic dinner. She arrived right on time and my husband called to let me know he was on his way home. Things started to look up.

I decided to crack open the wine while I was waiting for him so it could "breathe," not to mention the fact that I really needed a drink. Turns out, the wine didn't just breathe, it "gasped" as I splintered the cork into a hundred pieces. I grabbed my colander and started pouring the wine into it over the sink, catching the now cork-free liquid in a plastic pitcher. I wondered if this is what they would do at a fine dining establishment if they had this problem. Then I realized, chances are, they probably wouldn't have this problem.

After pouring myself a glass of wine, I started to heat the french onion soup in the microwave. While it was cooking, I could hear all sorts of snap, crackles, and pops. I didn't think much of it until I opened the microwave door to retrieve the soup and was greeted by something straight out of a science fiction movie. Apparently, the plastic container the soup was in wasn't microwave safe and it had melted, spilling its contents all over the bottom of the microwave and onto the floor.

As I was cleaning up this miserable mess, my husband walked in and greeted me with a big smile and a beautiful bouquet of flowers. He couldn't figure out why I greeted him with a snarl rivaling that of the rabies-ridden *Cujo*. Can't you just feel the love?

After I withdrew my protruding fangs from his leg, I began to heat up round two of our dinner. It was filet mignon and I made sure I put it on a proper microwavable dish. Fortunately, this mighty morsel of moo-cow (as my two-year old would say) survived its plight and was actually quite tasty.

After enjoying some dessert and coffee, we blew out the candles on the table and headed for the couch to snuggle and watch a little TV. I realized this romantic interlude would soon come to an end when I looked over at my husband who was sound asleep next to me.

Well, it may have not been the Valentine's Day every woman dreams of, but you know what? As I stared over at my husband's peaceful face, I couldn't help but smile.

Can't you just feel the love? I can.

Valentine's Day — Lost in Translation

Did anybody ever stop to consider why we celebrate Valentine's Day? One legend contends that Valentine was a priest who served during the third century in Rome. When Emperor Claudius II decided that single men made better soldiers than those with wives and families, he outlawed marriage for young men. Valentine, realizing the injustice of the decree, defied Claudius and continued to perform marriages for young lovers in secret. When Valentine's actions were discovered, Claudius ordered that he be put to death.

Translation: We're celebrating the fact that a priest secretly married those in love and was then killed for it. Hmmmm, doesn't exactly make me feel all warm and fuzzy inside.

I don't think Valentine's Day is a holiday my husband feels all warm and fuzzy about either, but he certainly puts up a good front. He knows I love romance and always tries to make the day special for me. This year he actually started early in the week when I was watching the *Bachelorette*. Usually when this show is on he stays clear, but this particular night as he was doing the military crawl on his belly across the kitchen floor to get a drink, I stopped him dead in his tracks.

"See how he's looking at her. Why can't you look at me that way?"

"What do you mean? I look at you like that all the time."

"Yeah, let's see it."

Slowly, he rose to his feet, grabbed me around the waist, tilted his head to the side, and stared deep into my eyes.

"Well, I appreciate the attempt, but that was more like a deer caught in the headlights."

Translation: Husband + Romantic Gaze =
Scary Proposition

Like I said, he gets an "A" for effort, but it wasn't quite what I was looking for. Valentine's Day was still a couple of days away so he had time to redeem himself.

February 14th - 7:30 a.m.

I came downstairs and was greeted by three pairs of blue eyes.

"What are you doing here?" my husband asked. "Go back upstairs. We're making you breakfast in bed." I wasn't going to argue with that, so back I went.

8:00 a.m.

Just as I started to drift back to sleep …

"I wanna watch the *Wiggles*."

"I hate the *Wiggles*."

"That's it, we're turning off the TV."

"WAAAAAHHHHHHHH!!!!!"

Suddenly, two sobbing little boys were cuddling up next to me in bed while my husband was hot on their heels with a breakfast tray.

"C'mon guys, get out of the bed. And by the way, honey, Happy Valentines Day!" <SLAM>

Now *that* makes me feel all warm and fuzzy inside.

10:30 a.m.

After things calmed down, my husband took the boys outside to let me have a little alone time. A few minutes later I heard…

"WAAAAAAAAAHHHHHHHHHH!"

"What happened?"

"We just sledded into a tree."

I looked out the window and there was my eldest son, blood streaming from his mouth. Upon closer inspection, I could see he had bitten his lip.

Translation: Husband + Babysitting = Injury, TLC, and a Popsicle

7:30 p.m.

After putting the kids to bed, I came down to a room full of candles and the smell of a lovely home-cooked meal. My husband had prepared it all by himself and gracefully greeted me with, "Happy Valentine's Day, dear. I love you. By the way, you might want to eat a lot of the appetizer 'cause the steak is kinda like a hockey puck."

Translation: Husband + Kitchen = Sensory Surprise

9:00 p.m.

After cleaning up, we decided to relax and watch the movie, *Lost in Translation*, with Bill Murray. We had both heard good things about it, however, after two hours of phasing in and out of consciousness, we decided it was a little slow and definitely "lost in translation" on us. Or as my husband so eloquently put it, "This movie stinks."

I really do appreciate my husband's attempt at creating romance for me on Valentine's Day, but somehow I think my idea of romance gets lost in the translation. Regardless, my husband is still my favorite Valentine and I think next year I'll make it a little easier on the poor guy.

Translation: Husband + Valentine's Day 2006 = a kiss, a card, and take out.

Chapter 8
On Vacation—Wish I Weren't Here

Like the holidays, vacations are supposed to be a time when families spend quality time together—a time to pack up and go somewhere to get out of the rut of their everyday routine. I get the whole concept, but unfortunately this hasn't been the case during our vacations over the past couple of years. I usually feel like I need a vacation from my vacation when I get home.

I recognize my viewpoint may be a little tainted since some people have mentioned I'm perhaps a little "tightly wound"—OK downright uptight—but I still can't help but wonder if other people might feel the same way if they were in my shoes. You be the judge.

Camping—A Learning Experience

We just came back from a camping trip to Hermit Island in Bath, ME. It was the first time camping with our boys, and let's just say—it was a learning experience. This is what we learned.

Tarpé Diem — Tarp early and tarp efficiently. We learned this after a pretty hefty thunderstorm dampened our campsite. My husband had put up a tarp the day before the storm, but it wasn't quite big enough to do the job. When the storm hit, the winds lifted this puppy right off its posts and flew it around like a flag on the fourth of July.

As my husband scrambled around to get it under control, I

calmly informed him that there was a small lake forming under our tent. Throwing the tarp into the air, he ran over and started feverishly digging trenches to divert the water. It didn't work. The result—a soggy tent floor. Wouldn't be so bad if we were fish, but sleeping in a puddle the size of a small lake isn't my idea of a good time.

You're only as good as your last hors d'oeuvre — One of the reasons we went on this trip was because my brother-in-law and his family had been going for years with about ten other families and they loved it. It was a great group of people and you could tell they knew how to have a good time. Every day at 4:30 p.m. they would have happy hour on the beach. The women would supply the hors d'oeuvres while the men supplied the cocktails. My sister-in-law informed me of this daily event, so I was prepared—well, sort of.

I had brought the basics: chips and salsa, cheese and crackers, veggies and dip. Nothing fancy—it was camping, right? Wrong. As I was offering my meager morsels, I watched in horror as the other women approached with delectables that looked like Emeril had just whipped them up. BAM—fresh salmon. BAM—bruschetta. BAM—oysters on the half shell. It was embarrassing. I felt like the homely girl at the prom standing all alone in my light blue taffeta gown with everyone staring. Next year—prom queen.

Cooking over a fire is for rookies — When my husband and I used to camp we built a fire and cracked open a can of beans and other camp-worthy food. Not anymore. These folks fire up their gas grills and cook steak tips, swordfish, and other amazing eats. Note to self: "BUY GAS GRILL."

Tents are for the camping impaired — Sure, it was fun sleeping in a tent when we were wild and crazy and in our 20s, but now that we're 40 and have kids, sleeping on dirt doesn't have quite the same appeal. Most of the other people at the campground have already learned this lesson. Can you say, "pop-up camper?"

I don't want to give the impression that we didn't have any fun on this trip, because we did. I saw my first live starfish and crab. (Hey, I'm from upstate New York—give me a break.) My oldest son learned how to fish, and my husband took the boys out in a boat for the first time.

I'd like to chalk our vacation up to one of life's many wonderful learning experiences. It was great, but maybe next year we can experience—Bermuda!

You Call This Vacation?

Zip. Zip. Groan. Zip. Zip. Groan. Beep. Beep. Slam. Zip. Zip. Groan. Rustle. Rustle. Splash. Crunch. Crunch. Crunch.

"Honey, what are you doing?" my husband bellowed from the bowels of our army green tent.

"I'm eating breakfast—finally."

"But what was all that noise?"

"It was me *trying* to get out of my contortionist pose to exit my sleeping bag so I could flounder around and find the zipper that actually lets you out of the tent versus the one that toys with your head and just goes back and forth. Then, I was fumbling for the car keys to unlock the precious box of Fruit Loops hidden behind the alarm-protected car door. And, from there, Geraldo, to avoid the killer mosquitoes circling my head, I bravely dodged into the screen house so I could poke through these faint perforated lines on this miniature cereal box with my plastic spoon to unearth the crunchy morsels that lie beneath. I then smothered them with this milky white substance, which I believe is called milk, so I could devour them like any wide-eyed six-year-old would. By the way, did you say this was vacation or a casting call for *Survivor*?"

"Take it easy, honey. It's not that bad."

"Yeah, that's what I keep saying, but I can't quite hear myself through the sand, dirt, bug spray, and sunscreen clogging up my ear canal."

"Man, if I knew you were going to be this miserable, we wouldn't have come."

"Well, hello. I do vaguely remember hinting at that last year after we got back. Didn't you read my column?"

"Alright, alright, I got it."

"Just in case you missed it. Let me spell it out for you. Next year, I want R-O-O-M S-E-R-V-I-C-E!"

I'm really not the wicked witch of the deep dark woods, but I am ready to definitively come clean about something. I DON'T LIKE CAMPING!! I tried. I really tried. If you read last year's column you realize I had a little difficulty on a similar camping excursion. But, this year, I went into it with the attitude that I was going to correct the things that really bothered me. I pre-cooked a lot of our food so we didn't spend as much time cooking, I made sure I had snappy hors d'oeuvres for our group happy hour on the beach so I wasn't embarrassed, and I tried not to let the dirt and grime get to me. News flash—it got to me. It's official. I DON'T LIKE CAMPING!!

I'm not going to feel guilty about this admission, either. Other women I talked to feel the same way. As one of them so eloquently put it, "Going camping is essentially transporting your screaming children to a new location so that you can perform the drudgery of household chores outdoors without electricity or running water." Yeah, I'd say, that about sums it up.

Unfortunately, I didn't feel like I could share this viewpoint with my husband and sons before we left. They were too excited.

They don't care when creatures burrow into the dirt under their fingernails. They think that's cool. And, my husband, well, he couldn't wait to break out his new state-of-the-art gas grill, tarp that could cover the state of Texas, and four-foot tall Sterilite organizing drawers. I'm still not sure what he was organizing, but it made him happy. So, as you can see, it was hard for me not to "go along."

The only problem is, this was supposed to be my vacation too. And, according to my buddy, Webster, the word "vacation" is defined as, "a period of rest from work, study, etc." The key word here is "rest." DO I SOUND RESTED?

Call me crazy. Call me a baby. You can even call me a girlie-girl (which I'm definitely not), but for goodness sake, whatever you do, please, oh please, don't ever call me to go camping.

Summer Vacation — Part II

"Man, I'm exhausted. Drew was up four times last night," my husband explained with bleary eyes.

"I know. What was the problem?"

"Well, first it was a nightmare, then he couldn't find his stuffed animal, and I don't really know what it was after that. But you know what's weird? When I wasn't getting up to check on him, I dreamt that he bumped his head and it was bleeding."

"Yikes. Sounds like a nightmare."

"Yeah, I know. OK, I'm going to hop in the shower so we can get out of here on time."

"OK."

"Mommmmmmmeeeeee. Andrew just bumped his head. I didn't do it. I definitely didn't do it."

"Oh my gosh. He's bleeding. Mike, get down here. Your dream just came true."

"What?"

"Andrew bumped his head on the armoire and I think he needs stitches."

"Oh man, this isn't good. We're supposed to leave in 30 minutes for the airport."

"I know. Look, I'm going to take him to the doctor and you see if we can catch a later flight."

"OK."

And so started round two of our family vacation. I could just hear Murphy cracking up in his grave.

"Honey, the doctor said he can glue Drew's cut. No stitches. I think we can still make the flight so I'll meet you at the airport."

"OK. Sounds good."

Despite the drama, we were able to get to our flight on time. Things were looking up.

"Gee, we got through security pretty quickly. We should be boarding any minute now."

"Yeah."

"ATTENTION: We have an emergency in the building. Everyone must now exit the building immediately. I repeat. Please exit the building immediately."

"You've got to be kidding me."

"Mommy, what's going on?"

"There's some sort of emergency so we have to leave the building."

"But why?"

"Because they said so!"

OK, strike two. Three strikes and you're out, right? What was next? Hopefully, it wouldn't be as drastic as a terrorist attack, but I knew it would be something. Things always happen in threes.

"Ooh. Mommy, Andrew stinks."

"Shhh. Mike, do you think I can change him in that bathroom?"

"No way. It's like a closet. We'll have to wait until we land."

"But that's two hours from now."

"Ooh! Yuck!" my eldest interjected.

And, there you have it folks. Fortunately, once we reached our final destination of sunny Atlanta we had a lovely visit with my brother and sister and their families. But, between this experience and camping, I think next year I might just stay put and live up to the title my husband has bestowed upon me for being such a homebody.

Signed, yours truly, Bubble Girl.

Chapter 9
Miscellaneous Musings

This chapter contains columns that simply just "came to my brain" while observing the world around me. Perhaps they will make you ponder the things you encounter in everyday life. I know that since I've been writing my column, I always try to look at the humorous side of the things that normally drive me crazy. It makes for a much better day and a much more enjoyable life.

So, next time you're out and about with the kids and someone cuts you off on the highway, or the salesclerk at the store snarls at you, try to see the humor in the situation. It's always there if you look hard enough. Who knows, you might even laugh out loud— and that's a good thing!

Gee, You Haven't Changed a Bit

Well, we just returned from my 20th high school reunion. If you've been following my column, you know that I have been trying to lose weight for this "big event." The bad news is, I didn't quite reach my goal. The good news is, I wasn't the only one. But despite a few extra pounds, people kept telling me, "Gee, you haven't changed a bit." Whether they meant it or not, I'm not sure, but I found myself saying the same thing to others, and meaning it. Truth is, most of my classmates were just as I had remembered. Here's a recap of the weekend.

What to wear, what to wear? My mother had been asking me for months, "Did you buy a new outfit for the reunion yet?" Even though I wasn't really planning on it, I felt compelled to buy *something*. Since my idea of shopping generally involves ordering online from my buddies Eddie or L.L., I decided it would be in my best interest to take a couple of fashion-savvy friends to the mall with me.

As we entered the stores, my personal shoppers handed me articles of clothing I never would have considered, like—dresses. Yuck! That hasn't changed. I was a tomboy in high school, and I'm still a tomboy. After explaining I only wear these garments to weddings and funerals, we agreed on a pair of Capri pants and a sleeveless shirt, neither of which had ever seen the inside of my closet before. I always thought Capri pants were pants that never realized their full potential and avoided sleeveless shirts due to the "wave effect." You know, if I ever had to wave to someone, my upper arm might continue waving after my hand had stopped. This day, I decided to live dangerously.

When we got to the reunion, I was pleasantly surprised to see a lot of old friends and managed to say the right thing—most of the time. At one point, a fellow classmate walked by and as the memories came flooding back, I blurted, "You put gum in my hair in 9th grade." He glared at me, and kept walking. Oops!

Learning from my last outburst, I held my tongue when another classmate shared, "My undergraduate degree is in the study of lakes and I have a masters degree in the study of soil." What I wanted to say was, "Do you have a Ph.D. in the study of watching paint dry?" But, I kept my mouth shut.

As I looked around the room and talked with more people, it was like stepping back in time. The cheerleaders were still hanging out together and many of them had married the "jocks" they dated in high school. The smart kids were still having intellectual conversations that were way over my head, and the popular kids were still making sarcastic barbs about the not so popular kids. It was weird.

There were a few stories that no one would have predicted. The most dramatic tale came from my ex-boyfriend who was also our class president. Imagine my surprise when I found out that he had joined a monastery and became a monk. My friends joked that it was the demise of our relationship that pushed him into this profession. However, he reassured me that the influence came from someone a little further north with a tad bit more clout. And I don't think he was referring to Santa Claus.

Overall, I had a great time. It was great to see what everyone was doing, who they had married, how many kids they had, and basically to find out how they had attacked this thing called "life." In fact, people had such a good time, the organizing committee mentioned having a 25th reunion instead of waiting another 10 years.

Better start practicing. "Gee, you haven't changed a bit."

Ode to the Home-Based Working Mom

Other women often ask me how I made my decision to work at home and what it's really like. I try to share the good, the bad, and the ugly to give them a realistic perspective, but for me, it's easier to explain things by writing about it. As I was writing down my thoughts, I decided the way things seemed to unfold was kind of like a play entitled, *Ode to the Home-Based Working Mom.*

Scene 1: Workingwoman has her first child. From day one she looks at this bundle of joy with smiles, goo-goos, kitchy coos, and more. She enjoys her maternity leave (at least most of it), and then—reality hits. She has to go back to work. Part of her is happy about once again being able to have "adult conversation," but like the rest of us, she starts to sing the daycare blues. You know the tune—ear infections every other week, stomach flu on the opposite weeks, the smell of three different women's perfume on your child's clothes when you pick them up—the works. Still, for the good of the family's bottom line, superwoman continues to work, driving away from daycare each morning, tears streaming down her face, questioning, "What the heck am I doing?"

Scene 2: Workingwoman has baby #2. She's used to this daycare thing and decides to continue working. She drags herself to work each day to uphold the 70's badge of honor, "I am woman, hear me roar." Then one morning, when baby #2 decides mommy's suit would make a better diaper than the insignificant Pampers standing by, and baby #1 discovers the cat's back side, she has a brilliant idea. "I'll work from home. It will be PERFECT."

Scene 3: Turn the clock forward six months. "Tyler, get your hamster out of the toilet. Andrew, put your clothes back on. No, not you Mr. Sanders, I was talking to my son. No, I'm really not too busy to take on this project. When do you need it? Tomorrow? Sure, no problem (click). Boys—c'mon get the cat out of the microwave."

Perfect, right? Yeah, welcome to the world of the "home-based working mom." What does that mean exactly? It should be more like the "home-based, keep your kids from killing the cat, streaking across the front lawn, discovering permanent marker on the wall is indeed permanent, stay up 'till 3:00 a.m. to finish a $50,000 project, mom."

So, what do you do now? Go back to work? No, never. That would be admitting defeat. My advice—ENJOY! You see, I too have traded a closet full of $200 suits for a drawer full of sweatpants and shirts that have served themselves not only as garments, but also as tissues, napkins, and other orifice wiping mechanisms and love every minute of it.

Fear not, my friends. After being home for almost six years, I'm happy to say it was the right choice. Each day I'm home to experience my kid's accomplishments, failures, and even illnesses, I know I made the right decision. These moments are irreplaceable. You can go back to the corporate world anytime (although I doubt you will). Throughout the dirty diapers, the temper tantrums, the embarrassing moments at the grocery store, it's all worth it.

Holy Pet Debt, Batman

My husband and I have just decided to take out a second mortgage on our home. Not because the rates are good, not because we're planning on doing more renovations, but to cover the bills we've recently amassed at the veterinarian's office.

Over the past two months, we've taken our cats, Fred and Barney, to the vet three times.

The first time was for their annual checkup and rabies boosters. It was then that it was discovered that both cats needed some additional "maintenance."

First, the vet informed us that Barney had a cavity. How the heck did that happen? Was he sneaking candy from my hidden stash? Did he jump on the ice cream truck and consume too many Nutty Buddies? Who knows? All we knew was that the humane thing to do would be to have the cavity filled. Actually, the real humane thing would have been to have it filled last year when the vet first told us about it. But since he wasn't complaining, well…

When we went to pick Barney up, the receptionist handed me a bill with a figure that looked very similar to our monthly car payment. I thought if I stared at this numerical nightmare long enough one of the zeros hanging off the end would magically drop off. I was wrong. After playing tug-of-war with my credit card (the receptionist won), I looked down to see how my money was spent. All I saw was a groggy, cross-eyed cat in a brown plastic box looking up at me with eyes like daggers. I was quickly overwhelmed with a severe case of post-purchase dissidence.

Then it was Fred's turn. At first, we were quite embarrassed to take him to the vet because his fur was so matted it looked like he had dreadlocks. It wasn't the sort of haircut that suited his aloof feline personality. You know the type—the typical cat that swings open the front door donning a Frank Sinatra fedora with a trench coat slung over his shoulder, demanding an ice-cold kitty martini. That's Fred. We thought for sure the vet would call DKS (Department of Kitty Services) and report our grooming negligence. Instead, he commented, "Oh, it looks like Fred hasn't been cleaning himself too well." Phew, we were off the hook.

Just the same, we decided to have the vet shave Fred's fur for a more appropriate look. I had visions of him coming home completely shaved except for his big fluffy head. This vision quickly changed when my husband called and said, "I just talked to the vet. They were able to tease out most of Fred's mats so they don't have to totally shave him." Suddenly, my vision changed to that of three beauty school dropouts from *Grease*, breaking out into song as they teased his fur with large, bright pink combs.

Needless to say, he wasn't happy when we went to pick him up. My son asked, "Why's Fred so mad?"

I responded, "He's just having a bad hair day." That was an understatement. And the cost for this feline fiasco—$55. More than I pay for a cut and a color without the benefit of sedation.

The sad truth is, since our kids were born, our cats have kind of become second-class citizens. At times, I feel a little guilty about this, but when I see Fred drinking out of the toilet and Barney sucking on our toothbrushes, the guilt subsides rather quickly.

Well, we've paid the vet bills and we still have the cats, but I think my husband and I both agree that these are the last pets we'll ever own. That was until last week when my son uttered six words that made us both cringe, "Mommy, can we get a dog?"

Minivan Rap

I'm not really a fan of rap music, but I do appreciate the poetry and rhythm of some of the lyrics. The only problem is, a lot of the songs are about teen angst or relationships gone bad, things I really can't relate to. I decided to write my own rhythmic prose about a topic that is a little more familiar to me and to other parents of young children. So, here it goes…

As I'm driving down the road in my hip minivan,

I look in the rear view to see where I've been.

My sons are safely locked in their seats in the back,

Crunchin' away on their snackity snack.

Now son number one says, "Hey Mom, here's my trash,"

Around my arm reaches as I try not to CRASH.

Then son number two says, "Hey, me, too,"

Back goes my arm as he hands me some, "OOOhhhh!"

We're cruisin' along, smilin' ear to ear,

Until my baby drops his dinosaur and cries for a year.

Again I reach back, this time to retrieve,
The T-rex dinosaur from *Land Before Time III*.

Everything seems OK; we're still going strong,
Until my eldest screams, "Mommy, something's wrong."
I turn to the right to see my son's face,
It's as white as my favorite Laura Ashley pillowcase.

The next thing I know, I hear a nasty sound,
I'll spare you the details, but lunch was now on the ground.
We rolled down the windows to try and get air,
Where should we go? To home, that's where.

It seemed like forever in this home on four wheels,
My son was now green as I sighed, "What's the deal?"
Trying to hurry and get these kids home,
"Slow down," said a cop through his big megaphone.

I pulled to the side as he got out of his car,
He asked for I.D., and of course I said, "Yes, sir."
As he called the stop in, my sons started to bicker,
The stench and the tension just got thicker and thicker.

I looked to the heavens and said a quick prayer,
"Please God, get me home, this is a total nightmare."

The policeman wrote a warning and scolded me a bit,

I'm off again home, first slow, and then quick.

Alas we arrive at our beautiful home,

A sight for sore eyes, "Thank Goodness," I moan.

To bed goes my son, in hopes of getting well,

The "lunch" will have to wait, I can't bear the smell.

It's time for this minivan rap to come to a close,

I'm the Mommy from Groton writin' her minivan prose.

Don't worry, I've decided it's not my destiny,

But it sure was fun to be a rapper "wannabe."

I Know It's Spring When...

Officially spring starts March 21st, but in my house, there are other signs that more clearly indicate when the season has begun.

For instance, I know it's spring when…

I go to watch my son's first soccer game and while sitting on the sidelines admiring the piles of freshly cut grass, I realize I'm actually sitting in dried goose poop recently revealed by the spring thaw.

I go out for my morning jog through the woods, where during the winter the only things in sight are the snow covered branches and small fauna searching for food. Now, just as I take my inconspicuous runner's spit (and all runners know what I'm talking about), a bike rider approaches from behind and catches me spewing in full view. The only good thing is that I'm sweaty and disheveled enough to be beyond recognition so hopefully I won't be hearing that person in the local grocery store saying, "You know that humor columnist? Well, I just saw her..." Not the sort of recognition *this* writer is looking for.

I drive by the bus stop and see teenagers waiting for the bus in shorts and tank tops clearly mistaking these balmy 50-degree spring days as an instant rite of passage to ditch the corduroys and cable knits or any other form of attire that fully covers the appendages.

I can finally unearth the orange extension cord winding through the yard and up the drainpipe that once powered the Christmas lights.

My husband gets that glint in his eye that says, "Watch out, lawn, here I come," as he drops a truck load of fertilizer, grass seed, and various other Herculean lawn care products on the floor of the garage.

The cat leaves a dead mouse on the porch and proudly stands over it with paws on hips announcing the return of hunting season and of the ferocious feline predator.

The squirrels heckle me through the window as they eat the food from the bird feeder that was once out of their grasp due to the slippery icicles left by Father Winter.

We go to Disney World for spring break and the nicely bronze native Floridians quarantine us because of our ill-looking pasty white winter complexions.

Our social calendar resembles a missile war plan, various colors mapping out all of the children's spring activities.

I replace the license plate on our minivan with one that simply states, "Taxi," to take the children to above activities.

My husband claims he is leaving the house early for work, but the clinking sound of golf clubs rattling around in his trunk as he drives away is a clear indication he has something else in mind.

I call the kids in for dinner after playing outside, and realize there are three of them sitting across from me. The problem—to the best of my knowledge—I only gave birth to two.

Yes, spring is upon us and I'm sure many people are enjoying it. Unfortunately, I'm not one of them. Why? I just caught a glimpse of my naked body in the mirror, realized swimsuit season is right around the corner, and crawled back into bed for the next six months. Oh well. See you in the fall!

Moms in the Hood

Recently, a couple of my friends told me they are tiring of their weekly playgroup and want to "jump ship." The only problem is, they fear the potential ramifications of their departure. Will the other women ever speak to them again? Will they be black balled from joining the PTA? Will the children bombard them with Dunkin' Munchkins as they make their exit? It's almost as if they are a member of a gang and they can't "jump out" because the pull of the gang is too strong and the potential consequences of leaving the gang are too great.

For those of you who might not be familiar with the concept, a playgroup is basically a group of mothers and their young children gathering together at an agreed upon location, usually one of the mother's homes. The mothers drink coffee while the children play harmoniously nearby. It's an opportunity for both mother and child to socialize with their peers and build life-long relationships. It's really a great concept—in theory.

"Suzy, why are you crying?"

"Billy pulled my hair—really, really hard."

"Did not."

"Did too."

"Did not."

"Did too."

This is one type of altercation that typically takes place. And then, it's not long before…

"Mom, Ricky put my hamster in the toilet."

"I just wanted to see if it could swim. It can't. Stupid hamster."

And so it goes. The harmonious sounds of children playing nearby turn into the shrieks of battling toddlers trying to prove their proverbial "pecking order" in this unlikely suburban version of gang life. After a few weeks of this "in-fighting" it's no wonder my friends want to head for the hills (or therapy, as the case may be). But, it's also no wonder they fear what might happen after they depart.

"Can you believe Mary left the playgroup?"

"No. Does she think she's better than us?"

"Who knows, but I'm not letting Johnny play with Danny anymore."

"Me either."

It's this "gang mentality" that is really frightening. It starts when the playgroup is forming. In order to "jump in" or join, you must prove yourself worthy of belonging. In the gang world, this generally means behaving badly to prove you are just as tough as the gang members. In the playgroup world, you must prove your toughness by hosting the playgroup, serving award-winning apple strudel, and remaining composed when Jimmy spills grape juice on your pristine white sofa—the smallest flinch could end your chance of ever becoming a member.

Then, there is the uniform. In gang life, members generally don like-colored baseball caps or bandanas to show their allegiance. In playgroups, the wardrobe of choice is stretch pants, white turtleneck, and sweatshirt stating, "World's Best Mom" or something equally as trite. And at holiday time, the ever-so-lovely festive cardigan replaces the sweatshirt, the more pumpkins or snowmen the better.

Some playgroups even come up with names for their group, similar to gangs. An infamous gang name—the "Crips." An infamous playgroup name—the "Cribs."

The vehicles gangs and playgroups travel in are equally notable. While gang members might cruise in a rusty Cadillac with bass-shaking tunes blaring from the oversized woofers in the trunk, members of a playgroup cruise the "hood" in colorful minivans blaring, "The Wheels on the Bus," from their crude cassette deck.

I feel bad for my friends trying to break free. It seems like an impossible task. Maybe it would be easier for them to get kicked out. You know, "get them before they get you."

"Mary, this, uh, devils food cake tastes a little funny."

"Oh, really."

"Yeah, and my stomach isn't feeling that great."

"Hmmm. I'm sorry."

"Me too. Where's your bathroom?"

"Right down the hall on the right. Danny, why don't you take out your finger paints and do some painting with the kids."

"OK, Mommy."

"Mommy, Danny is painting scary pictures and won't stop saying, "Red Rum, Red Rum.""

{ALL CHILDREN SCREAM. MOTHERS GRAB CHILDREN AND MAKE A DASH FOR THE DOOR.}

"Leaving so soon?"

{NO ANSWER}

"Mommy, why did you want me to paint scary pictures and say, 'Red Rum, Red Rum?'"

"Oh, no reason honey, but you did a great job."

"Thanks, Mommy."

Mission accomplished!

Vote for Charlie Brown

I know politics is one of those taboo subjects that you're not supposed to talk about, but I think that's only at dinner parties and I'm not talking—I'm writing. So, here it goes.

First, let me stress that I have a great appreciation for our right to vote in this country and would not want to live anywhere else but the great U.S. of A. However, with that said, I must admit that I'm not a big fan of politics and find the voting process a little troubling and sometimes confusing. Let me explain.

The Candidates — My mother always taught me to try to get along with others. Although it didn't always work, I always gave it the ol' college try. I often wonder if politicians were taught the same thing by their parents. When I tuned in to watch the debate between two local politicians, Mitt Romney and Shannon O'Brien, I was hoping to walk away with some information to make a more informed decision at the polls. Instead, I walked away with this:

O'Brien: "You're Wrong."

Romney: "Am Not."

O'Brien: "Are too."

Romney: "Am Not."

O'Brien: "Are too. Infinity." Huh?

Gee, that cleared it up—NOT!

The Media Surveys — When it comes to the media surveys taken prior to the election, I'm skeptical of the accuracy of these predictions. You never know if the people they are asking are a fair representation of the public, and even if they are, you'll notice there is always some sort of *margin of error*. The last survey I saw before the election had Romney leading with a *margin of error of plus or minus 5%*. Imagine if you used this concept at home.

"Honey, where are my black pants?"

"In your top drawer. Of course, there's a margin of error of 5%. They could be anywhere. Good luck."

Doesn't seem too accurate, does it?

The Vote — Then there's the matter of voting. Choosing someone for the more publicized offices isn't too difficult because we've already been bombarded by information from the media. However, when it comes to choosing individuals for the less publicized offices, I find myself voting the same scientific way I pick football teams for my husband's office pool.

"Oh, that's a nice name. I'll vote for her." (check)

"Let's see. Oh yeah, I saw a picture of him. He's a nice dresser. I'll pick him." (check)

"I think he went to the same college as my friend, Beth. OK, I'll pick him." (check)

Hey, if a monkey can beat out a stockbroker at picking stocks, then maybe my methods aren't so crazy.

The Ballot — Then there's the issue of the physical ballot. Fortunately, we don't have to worry about those funny things called "chads" (whoever he is) like the voters in Florida, but I still find myself struggling with completing the ballot correctly. This year, when I came home to discuss who I voted for with my husband, I realized something.

"You know, I didn't see those questions on the ballot about x, y, and z. Why is that?"

My husband, always a patient man, simply looked at me and said, "Did you turn the ballot over?"

Oops!

I'm going to work on my voting ineptness, but if I find I'm struggling at the next election, I think I'll save myself and the candidates the agony and simply write in a vote for Charlie Brown. What the heck? He's honest, he's loyal, he's a snappy dresser, and it wouldn't be the first time a blockhead was voted into office.

About the Author

Kathryn Mahoney has been entertaining friends and family with her humor for years, but it wasn't until after the birth of her second child that she decided to "share." In 2001 she began writing her column, "Sunny Side Up," for Nashoba Publishing of Devens, MA, and continues to write for them today.

Kathryn is also a regular columnist for SanityCentral.com and has had her column published on a variety of parenting Web sites, as well as in the book *Misadventures of Moms and Disasters of Dads.*

When Kathryn isn't busy writing her humor column, she's running her business CreativEdge Marketing Communications out of her home in Groton, MA, where she resides with her husband and their two sons.

We empower mom writers.

Publishing the Works of Extraordinary Mom Writers

Wyatt-MacKenzie Publishing, Inc

WyMacPublishing.com